WITH MY SHIELD

OSPREY
PUBLISHING

WITH MY SHIELD

AN ARMY RANGER IN SOMALIA

SHIELD

JAMES LECHNER

OSPREY PUBLISHING
Bloomsbury Publishing Plc
Kemp House, Chawley Park, Cumnor Hill, Oxford OX2 9PH, UK
29 Earlsfort Terrace, Dublin 2, Ireland
1385 Broadway, 5th Floor, New York, NY 10018, USA
E-mail: info@ospreypublishing.com
www.ospreypublishing.com

OSPREY is a trademark of Osprey Publishing Ltd

First published in Great Britain in 2023

A catalog record for this book is available from the British Library.

ISBN: HB 978 1 4728 6328 7; PB 978 1 4728 6329 4; eBook 978 1 4728 6324 9;
ePDF 978 1 4728 6325 6; XML 978 1 4728 6326 3

23 24 25 26 27 10 9 8 7 6 5 4 3 2 1

Plate section image credits are given in full in the List of Illustrations (pp. 6–7).
Maps by www.bounford.com

Index by Zoe Ross

Typeset by Deanta Global Publishing Services, Chennai, India
Printed and bound in Great Britain by CPI (Group) UK Ltd, Croydon, CR0 4YY

Contents

List of Illustrations   6

Maps   8

Preface   10

Introduction   17

1   Seed Corn   21

2   Climbing the Mountain   49

3   Steel Sharpens Steel   65

4   Drumbeat   105

5   On the Hunt   141

6   Into the Valley   179

7   Storm of Steel   199

8   Borne the Battle   243

Epilogue   275

Index   281

LIST OF ILLUSTRATIONS

My parents, Jim and Sally, and I at The Citadel, Charleston South Carolina on Ring Night, 1988. (Author's collection)

The author serving as the fire support officer for Alpha Company, 3rd Battalion, 75th Ranger Regiment. pictured in front of a Ranger RSOV, or gun jeep, in 1991. (Author's collection)

Rangers from Alpha Company doing SPIE (special purpose insertion/extraction) rig from a Black Hawk helicopter during training at Elgin Air Force Base, Florida, in 1992. (Author's collection)

Alpha Company fire support team (FIST), with the author at the right and Butch Galliete second from left. (Author's collection)

Heavily armed Rangers sit on the edge of the doorway of Super 64 over Mogadishu. (Author's collection)

A picture taken by the author from Super 64 while flying over Mogadishu in September 1993. Note the task force helicopters over the city in the distance. (Author's collection)

Rangers riding inside Super 64 during a mission over Mogadishu, Captain Mike Steele is pictured in the center. (Author's collection)

The route taken by the assault force, including the author,
   from the target building to the Super 61 crash site.

Bravo Company, 3rd Battalion, 75th Ranger Regiment, in
   the desert outside of Mogadishu in September 1993.
   (Author's collection)

The only picture taken from the ground during the battle.
   Shown is the target building and Rangers of Chalks One
   and Four in the street in security perimeter. (Author's
   collection)

The Chief of Staff of the U.S. Army, General Gordon
   Sullivan, pins the Purple Heart on the author at Walter
   Reed Army Medical Center in October 1993, as his wife
   Beth and sister Amy look on. (Author's collection)

The author and Arnold Schwarzenegger at Walter Reed
   Army Medical Center, October 1993. (Author's
   collection)

The author and President Bill Clinton at Walter Reed Army
   Medical Center, October 1993. (The White House)

Members of Task Force Ranger stand in formation in front of
   the tactical operations center at Mogadishu Airport at a
   memorial service for their fallen comrades following the
   battle on October 3. (Courtesy 75th Ranger Regiment)

Mike Durant being carried to a medical evacuation aircraft
   by members of Task Force Ranger after his release
   in Mogadishu. (Courtesy US Special Operations
   Command)

The author's combat boot on display at the National Infantry
   Museum, Fort Benning, Georgia. This was worn when
   he was wounded on October 3, and the bloodstain shows
   the depth of pool of blood. (Author's collection)

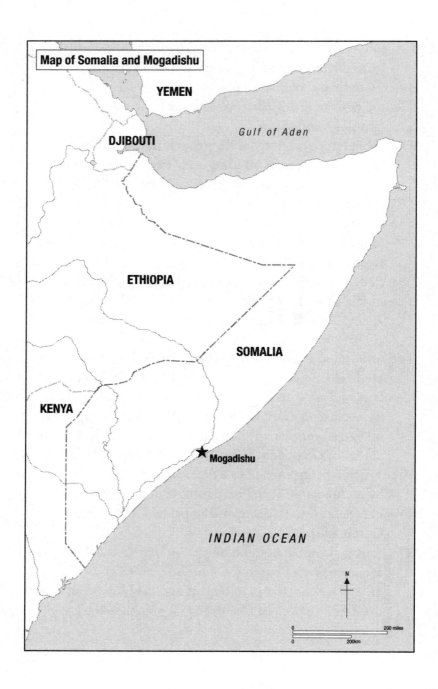

Map of Somalia and Mogadishu

YEMEN

Gulf of Aden

DJIBOUTI

ETHIOPIA

SOMALIA

KENYA

★ Mogadishu

INDIAN OCEAN

N

0   200 miles
0   200km

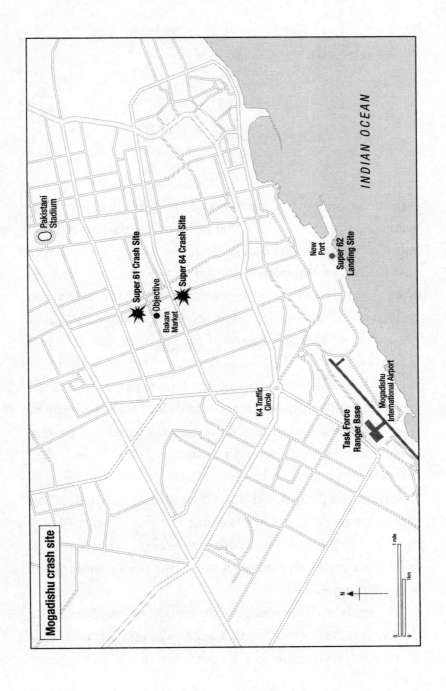

Mogadishu crash site

Pakistani Stadium

Super 61 Crash Site

Objective

Super 64 Crash Site

Bakara Market

New Port

Super 62 Landing Site

K4 Traffic Circle

Mogadishu International Airport

Task Force Ranger Base

INDIAN OCEAN

N

1 mile

1km

PREFACE

The creation of this book was a process of nearly four years in the making. It was a process that paralleled my evolving understanding over the years of the battle itself. One of the perceptions that I have come to over time is that everyone who participated in the battle can only truly attest to what happened in the immediate area around him. That boundary of reality is measured in just a few feet. Beyond the diameter of what an individual could physically touch during the battle, perception often became hazy, misunderstood, and the facts unknown. This becomes apparent whenever two veterans sit and discuss the battle, comparing notes on their experience. Nearly every time I have personally done this I have learned something I did not know about the battle. The same is true of not only writing the manuscript of my personal experience but also researching the battle to provide a more complete picture and understanding of what happened.

The initial writing was in many ways the easiest part. The double porches of my South Carolina plantation provided an idyllic and quiet haven to draft the initial manuscript.

The story, so oft repeated, seemed to easily flow out onto the pages and was finished in a matter of weeks. But like the story, or more accurately the more complete picture of the battle, the process of crafting, editing, and completing the manuscript took far longer.

For years since 1993, I had been repeating the story, usually in classrooms, lecture halls, and auditoriums. During these presentations I would flesh it out with standard anecdotes and my own memories of the battle. But as I began to closely scrutinize the manuscript with the assistance of other veterans of the battle and sharp editors, I began to look at it more critically with the eye of a historian. Through this research I was able to not only correct some misconceptions but also bring to light a number of key things and establish sequences of events which were not previously known or clearly understood.

I am greatly indebted to the numerous individuals who have provided advice, feedback, and formal editing. Numerous fellow veterans of the battle took their time to compare memories and verify events. Among the many veterans of the battle who gave me their perspectives, I am indebted to Mike Steele, Scott Spellmeyer, Rick Lamb, Keni Thomas, Raleigh Cash, and Mike Goodale. I also learned a great deal reading the monographs from Tom DiTomasso and Lee Ryswyk of their experiences in 1994, written at the Infantry Officers Advanced Course. My friend and teammate from Afghanistan, J.D. Stevens, related important details he learned from the Somali leader (and one of our targets) Osman Atto, after befriending him in Mogadishu years later.

Especially helpful among the aviators of the 160th SOAR were Hal Wade and Chuck Harrison. It was not until decades later while listening to Stan Wood relate his story as a pilot during the battle, that I learned many new things about the experiences of the TF 160 helicopter crews. More importantly, I saw color video from the battle that proved some of my memories were in error. An example of this is my seemingly clear memory of approaching the target building from the west aboard Super 64 on October 3. However, the video clearly shows that, in reality, we approached from the north. In truth I had become disoriented during the flight. To this day, in my mind I still clearly see the approach under that misconception.

As is so often the case, I owe many individuals my thanks in making this book a reality. D.D. Spivey gave it the first professional editing. I met D.D. through her late husband, my fellow US Army veteran and friend Stephen Spivey, as we worked on the Afghanistan documentary *Fallen Angel* in 2019. Her patience and professional eye moved the manuscript smoothly forward. When so many trails for publication of the manuscript had led to dead ends, Joseph Craig and the Association of the United States Army got it back on track and set it on the path to success. Marcus Cowper and the team at Osprey took it the final lap and did amazing work with further editing and significant improvement, along with critical fact checking. I would also like to mention Bill Powell, Carlos Rodriguez, Mike Moser and BAJ. Of all the battles I have been a part of, Mogadishu seems to be exceptionally cloaked in the fog of war. The shades of gray continue to distort perceptions. Despite the assistance and efforts of so many to bring this book to fruition, any errors found are solely my responsibility.

My family have always been the sea upon which I sail, keeping me afloat during the storms while also serving as the beacons to guide me home. Along with my daughters Carolina, Catey, and Sarah, my wife Beth is certainly the singular embodiment of that sentiment. She recently noted we have now been married longer than we were single. But her golden thread seems to have always been woven into the story while I was in Somalia and especially after I returned home from there badly wounded. The support of a family, and especially a wife, cannot be underestimated for a soldier at war. In some ways their burden is greater under the weight of the unknown and fear of the unexpected knock at the door, which they try to hold at arm's length. Beth bore this with amazing grace and continues to do so. In 1993 when she was turning 21, being a newlywed, an expectant mother, and then nursing a wounded soldier within the span of six months was not a fairytale envisioned by any young woman. Beth's perseverance and character under those conditions, largely unsung, are a marvel to all those who know her.

In this information age which often seems to revel in exposé, self-aggrandizement, and victimization, I hope I will be indulged in this memoir for what it is, or at least

13

hopes to be: an ode to the brotherhood of men in battle. It is a brotherhood begun with the time-transcending utility of severe training which builds the bonds, then seals them with the immortal honor of standing fast, shoulder to shoulder. War itself is not glorious but an abomination of humanity. The death, destruction, and human wreckage of the battlefield ripples painfully not just through those who witness it, but echoes terribly for generations. However, similarly so does the example of living the life of a warrior and meeting the standards of a Ranger. As the Spartans said, "Come back with your shield, or on it." While my shield, the Lord Jesus Christ, lifts us for eternity above the parameters of our short existence, those who have stood in battle and not failed the men at their side stand forever as examples of the honor that rings through eternity.

Come back with your shield, or on it.

Spartan adage - Plutarch, *Moralia*: 241

The Lord is my strength and my shield;
in him my heart trusts, and I am helped...

Psalm 28:7

INTRODUCTION

As the early morning sun rose in the sky, the militiamen waited in their positions along the dusty, garbage-strewn road. Jiaalle Siaad Street was inside their Habr Gidr clan territory in southwest Mogadishu, the capital city of Somalia in the Horn of Africa. The militia of the Habr Gidr had begun fighting the military forces of the United Nations (UN) earlier that summer of 1993. In June, they had ambushed a patrol of Pakistani soldiers, killing 24 and massacring the wounded as they lay in the streets. Now, in early August, the Somalis were upping the ante. They were looking for Americans to kill and had observed them frequently patrolling here in their light HMMV trucks. The Somali gunmen had come before sunrise, clearing the street and digging the anti-tank mine into the road. There was little traffic now as the locals, wary of the impending attack, avoided the area. Soon, two U.S. Army HMMVs came into view. As the lead vehicle rolled over the mine, the militiaman pressed his detonator, tearing the light truck apart. Instantly, three Americans died and a fourth was mortally wounded. As the trail HMMV slammed to a halt, the Somalis engaged it with their AK-47 assault rifles, firing through the smoke and dust. The remaining U.S. soldiers radioed for help, trying to survive as they were pinned in position by Somali fire and blocked by the wreckage and smoking crater to their front. As the dust began to settle, nearby United Nations forces responded, arriving to assist the Americans and pick up the pieces as the militiamen faded away. Back in the United States, President Bill Clinton and the rest of the nation were shocked to receive the news of the ambush and American casualties. The President directed that action be taken and a long-contemplated U.S. military special operation was now put into motion.

The friction between the UN and the Habr Gidr clan, fronted by its political entity the Somali National Alliance (SNA), had been growing throughout the spring and summer of 1993. The first minor clashes and frictions began just months after the initial UN invasion of Somalia the previous December. That invasion came about when a group of nations, led by the United States, intervened militarily to secure the devastated failed state from the various warring tribal militias. This was of urgent necessity, as Somalia was also experiencing a severe famine and the UN needed to get in and on the ground to provide humanitarian aid to the starving refugees. Up to this point, the UN relief efforts had been blocked or plundered by the Somali militias, but the intervention of the UN military changed all of that and drove them into the shadows. While the rival militias initially faded into the background rather than confront the military forces of the UN coalition, the Somali National Alliance, one of the most powerful groups, had soon begun to look for opportunities to gain an advantage over their rivals. Driven by ambitions to gain power, some of the Somali militia, to include the SNA, also reacted in opposition to UN efforts to disarm them. The increasing resistance to the UN efforts by the SNA and their leader, former Somali general Mohamed Farah Aideed, were in part a response to raids mounted by the coalition's military forces to build greater long-term security. During these raids, the Habr Gidr neighborhoods were surrounded by UN troops, cordoned off, and searched in order to confiscate illegal weapons caches, heavy weapons, and armed trucks called "technicals." The SNA began to resist these raids and mount their own attacks on the UN troops that summer. These attacks included deadly street ambushes of Nigerian and Pakistani forces, in which scores of UN soldiers were brutally massacred and their bodies mutilated. In a growing cycle of violence, these Somali attacks were quickly followed by retaliatory raids primarily carried out by the U.S. military. On July 12, in response to the ambushes and hoping to crush the resistance and take out the SNA leadership, U.S. Army helicopter gunships targeted a large Habr Gidr clan meeting, inflicting devastating casualties. Unknown to U.S. forces at the time of the retaliatory air raid, the Somalis were discussing how to mitigate the growing conflict and depose Aideed. The strike on the clan meeting and resultant killing of tribal elders had only served to unify the Habr Gidr against the UN.

Now, after the killing of the four U.S. soldiers, orders flashed out from Washington to the elite Special Forces Operational Detachment–Delta (SFOP-D), Army Rangers, and the "Night Stalkers" of the 160th Special Operations Aviation Regiment (SOAR) to answer the call and begin to assemble in the pinelands of North Carolina at Fort Bragg.

That summer, I was a young Army lieutenant, serving with an infantry rifle company in the 3rd Ranger Battalion. August 1993 found our Ranger company training in the hot sands and rocky wadis of Fort Bliss, Texas, when we heard the news about the attack in Somalia. We could not have known that this explosion, on a dirty city street in Mogadishu, had not only killed four Americans but had triggered events that would reverberate through the United States military for generations.

My odyssey and the path that led me to Mogadishu would begin almost a decade before the attack on the American patrol. I had taken the first steps almost ten years before when I enlisted in the Army National Guard. On a cold January day at the recruiting station in downtown Rochester, New York, my father signed off on the required permission forms just a few weeks after my 17th birthday. Later that summer, after finishing my junior year in high school, I headed off to U.S. Army basic training at Fort Benning, Georgia.

I

Seed Corn

We must remember that one man is much the same as another,
and that he is best who is trained in the severest school.
Thucydides, History of the Peloponnesian War
(431–404 BC)

As the bus rolled past the digital thermometer on the south
Georgia interstate, I read 104 degrees in disbelief, thinking
something must be wrong with the sign. I had arrived at
Fort Benning, home of the United States Army Infantry
School, in the summer of 1984. Along with the rest of
the recruits, I stepped off the bus, blinking in the bright
sunlight, feeling the sticky heat soak into me. Set deep in
the South, Fort Benning in the summer is a vast furnace
of sand and pine trees where infantrymen, paratroopers,
and Rangers of the U.S. Army have been forged for over a
century. We were so new to the Army we still wore civilian
clothes as we milled around the parking lot of the trainee
reception station. We formed into long lines before being
stuck with needles, poked, prodded, and given reams of
paperwork with numerous codes printed across the bottom.

We would soon learn that these numbers represented the Army's internal administrative language. In the U.S. Army, every aspect of a soldier's life is broken down to a code and designated form number. You could follow the career of a soldier from beginning to end through this code and paperwork trail. A soldier's career begins with his enlistment on a DD4. He then makes major moves on a 4187. Finally, when a soldier's time in the Army is done, the trail ends with a DD214.

Sergeants informed us that we were now "trainees." We waited for hours to sign the endless documents handed to us by kindly Georgia natives who gave us sympathetic looks. After spending a quiet night locked down at the trainee reception station, we were taken the next day to the Fort Benning equipment issue facility. Located in a vast series of warehouses, it was packed with green and brown equipment of every description. Each trainee came out of the warehouse loaded down with two large duffel bags stuffed with uniforms, boots, socks, t-shirts, and other miscellaneous "kit."

Not long after we received our duffel bags full of gear and the last man exited the warehouses, we lined up again and packed into a small convoy of waiting buses. Sitting shoulder to shoulder in the cramped seats, we sweated in the July heat with our duffel bags piled on top of and around us as the buses pulled out of the reception station and headed farther out into the vast pine forests of Fort Benning. As we drove away from the main post, I saw signs pointing to "Sand Hill" out of the bus windows. Then, after just a few more miles, we pulled up in front of new brick "starship" barracks, so called for the wings of the building emanating out from the central headquarters. I did not have time to appreciate the architecture, as a seemingly irate drill sergeant hopped onto the bus even before it had completely stopped. His main issue seemed to be the fact that we were still in our seats, with our bags piled on top of us. With loud directions and intense encouragement, we streamed out of the buses and into the parking lot. Here, the drill sergeants forcefully introduced order into the chaos as we were broken down from a milling mass of recruits into platoons of 40 men.

The trainee platoon to which I now belonged was the typical cross-section of America, from inner-city Blacks and Hispanics to Kentucky hillbillies. We would spend nearly every minute of the next nine weeks eating, sleeping, training, and working together in our platoons. We got to know each other well, and, while individual personalities carried on, especially among the recruits, it was my first experience with the true concept of a "melting pot." Wearing our uniforms, we all looked the same and our lives were regimented to the minute by the ever-present drill sergeants. The accents, attitudes, and many of the differences faded, giving way to the traditions and military culture of infantry soldiers.

Along with the rest of my platoon, I spent that summer as a young infantry trainee in loud, mostly one-way discussions with drill sergeants, tactics instructors, and infantry officers. They taught us the basic skills of the trade along with the lore and ways of the U.S. Army. In basic training, the U.S. Army's version of "boot camp," this mainly consisted of spending days and nights in the sandy hills and pine forests, marching, running, shooting weapons, digging foxholes, emplacing mines, learning first aid, and myriad other combat tasks. I walked for miles with the "ruck" on my back and carrying the rifle until it felt like part of my limbs. In basic training, we carried the M16A2 rifle, a slightly updated version of the weapon made famous during the Vietnam War.

Many of our leaders at Fort Benning were Vietnam veterans, as the last U.S. troops had left that war-torn country less than a decade before. As these veterans helped turn us into soldiers, they passed on lessons learned not only from the Army field manuals but also through their own combat experience. During basic training that summer, many of them inspired us by their example, leading from the front. One of these leaders was our brigade commander, Colonel Steve Siegfried. He had taken a machine-gun bullet through his hip in Vietnam and thus limped along, but he was always out in front of us on unit runs. At the same time, we caught occasional glimpses of some of the Army's newest combat veterans from the 75th Ranger Regiment, which was then forming at Fort Benning. An entire regiment of Rangers was being established by the Army, to include the newly formed 3rd Ranger Battalion.

This expansion of the Ranger Regiment was a direct result of the previously established 1st and 2nd Ranger Battalions having proven their value by successfully spearheading the invasion of Grenada less than a year prior. The first two Ranger battalions of the modern era had been formed less than a decade before, on the heels of the trauma in Vietnam, and now were simultaneously the Army's spearhead for combat operations and the leading force in its revitalization. These Rangers were role models and living icons, not only for young infantry recruits at Fort Benning, but for the entire Army.

Eight weeks after arriving at Fort Benning, I completed basic training and went back home to upstate New York to finish my senior year in high school. The Army had always been my dream, and this drove my decision to enlist in the Army National Guard. Now I was returning home after having my first real taste of the Army. My time at Fort Benning had been long, hot, and arduous, making that summer seem like two years, not two months. But it was not a question of whether I had "liked it," as my high school friends asked upon my return. Being a soldier was what I had always been destined to do.

Basic training was not designed to be enjoyed but endured, and it was where the Army started to winnow out the chaff. If you could get up before dawn, run for miles, then march all day in the heat and still be standing in the line that evening, then you could go on. I would go on and later return for more challenges and training at Fort

Benning. Each time I came back, it was to begin again, climbing to the next level: Infantry, Airborne, Ranger. I loved being a soldier, to pick up my rifle and carry the ruck. I loved being part of a team and standing shoulder to shoulder with other warriors. I also knew I wanted to lead other soldiers.

I grew up in the 1970s and '80s outside the city of Rochester, in the farmlands of upstate New York. Rochester was the home of Eastman Kodak and Xerox. It was 20th-century industry and new technology beside old farms and canal towns. My father, Jim, continued a long family tradition of working for Kodak, but had also done a four-year hitch in the U.S. Marine Corps before coming back to Rochester. My mother, Sally, was a nurse and came from a family of coal miners in Utah. My ancestors had been in America since before the Revolution, serving on both sides during the War for Independence. The Germans on my father's side served in the Pennsylvania militia under George Washington before coming to upstate New York. On my mother's side were English and Scottish Tories fighting for the King until being evacuated out of Philadelphia to Canada when the war began to turn against them. Later, others fought the British again in the War of 1812 before migrating west. Some of my ancestors followed the Mormon prophet Joseph Smith, riding in ox carts to Utah. Like so many in Rochester, my ancestors eventually included waves of Irish and more Germans in the 19th century.

Most families in Rochester had similar stories — immigrants and refugees hailing from all over Europe. Cherishing their second chance in America, their descendants were often patriotic, with many men having done their four-year stint in the military. When people asked me what I wanted to do after high school, they looked confused when I answered, "professional soldier." It seemed a foreign concept in a place where everyone worked for Kodak or went to the local college. I had grown up patriotic and loving history. In 1976, when I was in the fourth grade, we celebrated the Bicentennial at Florence Brasser Elementary School and my interest grew.

Growing up outside of Rochester, I did all the typical things boys do in small-town America. I played baseball in the summer and street hockey in the winter. With the local Boy Scout troop, I learned survival skills and how to live outdoors, camping year-round even in the harsh northern winters. Our Boy Scout troop was led by a dedicated, fatherly — but sometimes volatile — German immigrant. His own scouting experience had been in 1930s Germany with the Hitler Youth during the Third Reich. Wisely, his father had moved the family and escaped, eventually coming to America. On rare occasions, our Scoutmaster briefly mentioned the torchlit parades and huge rallies in Bavaria. He carried his "Blood and Honor" dagger on our camping trips, keeping the swastika carefully hidden under a thick wrapping of tape. Under his leadership and sometimes harsh discipline, our Scout troop sought extreme adventures and tough challenges. We hiked along the ruins of the Erie Canal and camped in the Adirondack Mountains. We took canoe trips over the same New York lakes and rivers navigated by Robert Rogers and his rangers when they had searched for the Northwest Passage and fought Indians 300 years earlier.

While my father came from a devout Catholic family in Rochester, my mother had been raised Southern Baptist, growing up in Illinois just outside St. Louis. In a twist of fate, or by God's hand, after her mother and sister were killed in a car accident, she had been sent back to Illinois from Utah. Toiling in the coal mines, my grandfather was unable to raise her by himself so my mother went to live with her uncle and his wife, a devout Baptist who took her to church. Being thereafter raised a Baptist diverted her path away from the Mormon tradition of our family in Utah. My mother ensured my sister and I attended church. We were members of a small Southern Baptist mission church in the inner city of Rochester. I would spend my childhood pulled between these two dogmatic Christian denominations: the devout Catholics of my father's family on one side and on the other the no-less-militant Southern Baptists of my mother's. I adapted, attempting to absorb the best of both faiths.

As a teenager in the early '80s, I attended Gates Chili High School where I excelled in history courses and played football with my best friend, Mike Jennings. Mike and I spent our weekends working various jobs and driving the streets of Rochester. I had planned to go to college after high school but increasingly felt compelled to pursue something else. I could still hear the drums of the Army and they were calling me back to the path I had started at Fort Benning.

Not long after my return from Fort Benning, watching television on a winter evening during my senior year in high school, I saw news coverage of a plane crash in Washington, D.C. A commercial airliner had come down in the Potomac River, slamming into the water between two bridges. Somehow, a few passengers had survived. As rescuers arrived, the survivors struggled in the deep, freezing water, trying to escape the wreckage. One passenger, Arland D. Williams, had made it to the surface but refused to come out of the water as he pulled other survivors from the plane and handed them rescue lines until he finally went down, succumbing to the cold. The news anchorman said Williams was a graduate of The Citadel, a military school in Charleston, South Carolina, "known for its harsh discipline, which had prepared him to be a hero." When I heard this story, my path became clear. Soon after, I visited South Carolina and The Citadel.

My flight lifted off from Rochester later that winter, leaving gray land and bare trees behind. At the airport, I saw David Henderson, the owner of the farm where I had worked in my small town. He was a gentle old sage who had spent decades at Kodak before retiring to the farm his family had owned for generations. His grandfather had carved "July 4th, 1876" into the massive oak door of their barn. Today, vacant shopping plazas stand over the farmland where Mr. Henderson's old barn, the door etched with history, used to stand. I often listened to Mr. Henderson talk about inevitable change and his worry that the local farming life was coming to an end. "Anyway, it's a hard life," he would say. "Winters too long and cold." That morning at the airport, I told him I was headed to Charleston, South Carolina, to visit The Citadel. He smiled knowingly and told me that he and his wife were off to Hawaii. Gray, snow, city blocks, farms — I left all of that behind as I headed south.

After landing at the airport in South Carolina, I left for The Citadel in a taxi, driving into the green, white, and old brick world that was Charleston. Coming through the main gates of the school, I knew I had never seen a place like The Citadel, with its white castles, towering palms and oaks, green parade deck, and prevailing sense of order and the Corps. It was a different world and from a different age than Fort Benning, but I knew with assurance that it was home for the next four years. Returning to New York, I rushed to apply for admission and was accepted that spring to The Citadel, Class of 1989. My acceptance letter came with a card with the letter "C" on it, representing my company assignment. The last page of the letter was a terse set of instructions to report in early August 1985, mere weeks after high school graduation.

Originally called the South Carolina Military Academy, The Citadel was established in the city of Charleston in 1842 along with The Arsenal in Columbia, which at that time was a satellite school for freshmen or Fourth Class cadets. Like many military academies established across the country at this time, the creation of The Citadel was inspired by the success of the United States Military Academy at West Point, which had opened less than two decades prior. Establishing an academy with a military system of education gave South Carolina a means to educate its young men and train future leaders. It also provided the state with a standing armed force, trained to deal with emergencies such as invasion, uprising or slave revolt in the antebellum period.

Years later, as the clouds of war gathered after the election of Abraham Lincoln in 1860, the cadets of the South Carolina Military Academy stood ready to respond to the orders of their leaders at the school and the Governor of South Carolina. When South Carolina seceded in December 1860, the cadets and their officers were ordered to emplace cannon and establish an artillery battery on Morris Island at the mouth of Charleston Harbor, joining other newly formed Confederate forces laying siege to Fort Sumter. That spring, in 1861, when President Abraham Lincoln sent the ship *Star of the West* to reinforce the fort, the cadet battery opened fire with its cannon. The ship was turned back as the cadets fired the first shots of the War Between the States. During the war, the cadets marched out of the gates of the school and fought as a corps on numerous occasions, earning nine battle streamers, which are carried to this day on the school's flag. The last one of these actions by the Corps of Cadets was a sharp firefight driving Union cavalry away from a railroad depot in the northern part of South Carolina in May 1865. This fight occurred after Lee had surrendered at Appomattox and weeks after Union General William T. Sherman had departed the state. It was the final action fought in South Carolina, making the Corps the "first and the last" in its defense.

In 1865, when the fortunes of war had finally turned against the South, the South Carolina Military Academy was closed before the advance of the Union Army under General Sherman. The Corps of Cadets picked up their rifles, formed into ranks, and departed, marching away to fight in defense of their homes. When the war ended, the Corps of Cadets was disbanded, and for ten years the school remained closed. Finally, the school in Charleston reopened as The Citadel. From these historic beginnings and this heritage as the post of honor in the service to their country, graduates of The Citadel have always carried on the proud traditions of the school. The marble and brass plaques in The Citadel chapel, inscribed with the names of "Our Patriot Dead," attest to the fact that Citadel men have been at the cutting edge of battle in every major military effort in defense of the nation.

Throughout a cadet's four years at The Citadel, he is subjected to exacting discipline, implemented through a military regimental system. This includes a daily schedule beginning with bugles at dawn, strict uniform codes, and rigorous standards of conduct and training, all tempered with the normal academic rigors of college. During my four years at The Citadel, the discipline of the Corps was pervasive and all-consuming. Most cadets were not allowed to possess civilian clothes while at school and, with the exception of special passes for the upper classes, cadets were restricted to the confines of campus 24 hours a day. The proud traditions of the Corps were sacred, enduring, and deeply entwined with the history of South Carolina. Every freshman cadet or "knob" was required to memorize the names of numerous battles, elegies of honor, prayers, and other lore of the institution. All of this was captured in one iconic symbol of the school: the Citadel ring. The ring encapsulated in gold the experience of every individual cadet and tied him indelibly to the Corps from its proud and honorable beginnings.

The Citadel class ring, like almost everything else at the school, was uniform and standardized with the exception of the class graduation year, and was referred to as "the Band of Gold." This ring was ceremoniously bestowed on the senior class in The Citadel's Summerall Chapel late in the fall semester each year. The ring marked Citadel graduates for life and was recognized not only in the military, but throughout the South and beyond. Young men came from every state in the nation and all over the world to join The Citadel Corps of Cadets. But before allowing young men to join its gray-clad ranks, The Citadel put them to the test. Beneath its exterior of gleaming white buildings, green drill fields, and the gold braid and brass of an afternoon dress parade, The Citadel was a ferocious test of endurance for freshmen of the Fourth Class.

The tradition of the Fourth Class system extends back through ancient times, enshrined in numerous modern military legacies such as the plebe system at West Point and military "boot camp" and recruit training such as I had experienced at Fort Benning. The system has its origins with the ancient Greek Spartans and their harsh Laconic system of training young men for war. Upon reaching a certain age in ancient Sparta, all young boys were taken from their families, formed into a class with their peers, and subjected to a harsh system of training called the *agoge*. The *agoge* system was characterized by brutal physical treatment, deprivation of food and sleep, and incessant military training. It was designed not only to build character and steel the hearts of the young men while preparing them for war, but also to develop the cohesion a group needed to resolutely stand fast in the shield wall or Spartan phalanx.

The success of the Spartan phalanx depended almost completely on each individual soldier doing his job and supporting the group. In the phalanx, an individual soldier carried a long spear held in his right hand and a large round shield with his left. His shield protected not only his own left side but also the spear arm and right side of his comrade standing in the rank close beside him to his left. If a soldier broke ranks or lowered his shield in battle, he would not only dishonor himself but expose and endanger his comrade. This type of training, then, has always been focused on developing the strength of the individual while also focusing on the cohesion and success of the group. By design, it is intended to find and break the "weak links" in training and winnow them out as the graduates of these systems go on to fight in defense of the nation. Failure in battle could well mean the death of both the unit and the nation. Today, 2,500 years later, the essence of combat — especially for infantry soldiers — has not changed fundamentally from that of their Spartan predecessors. The requirements of combat are unique and transcend any experience of civilized society, thus requiring a system of selection and training which is equally extraordinary. Viewed through the peaceful prism of a civilized society, this type of training system seems brutish, callous, and excessive. But there is a simple reason this harsh and exacting system has been around for over 2,500 years. It works.

Like the Spartan *agoge*, the Fourth Class or plebe system causes an individual to subordinate his personal well-being and comfort to the needs of the group by building discipline and character. In order for a young freshman to survive the Fourth Class system, he must reach down inside himself not only to endure, but also to persevere and contribute to the group, pulling his weight for his fellow classmates. This building of personal discipline and, more importantly, cohesion, ensures that he will never quit because to do so would let down his classmates and add to their burden as they struggle on.

While The Citadel was not the only military school to have a Fourth Class system at that time in the United States, it was arguably the toughest and most intense. It was unquestionably the longest, with the "knobs" of the freshman class enduring the Fourth Class system for the entire nine months of the school year.

Upon arrival at The Citadel to begin "knob" year, freshmen were dropped off outside the gates of their assigned barracks. Immediately upon setting foot inside the barracks, the new recruits entered into a carefully choreographed reception. Just steps inside the ironworks of the sallyport gate, on the red- and white-checkered quadrangle, awaited a glaring company cadet first sergeant sitting at a small table. The moment the newly arrived cadet recruit bent toward the table to sign his name on the roster, the cadet first sergeant sprang to life, bellowing harsh orders. This was the first of many shocks over the coming days, as each minute was regulated and regimented with drill, inspections, push-ups, and uniform changes. Freshmen were assigned to room with a classmate and, together, they lived in a small, spartan room that, despite its minimal furniture, included an open stand or full press for their uniforms, as well as bunk beds and two desks. They would work as a team to keep it in inspection order at all times. After the first few days, the schedule of in-processing for freshmen seemed to stabilize. One evening during their first week at the school, the cadet recruits in each company across the Corps were put down to bed by the late-evening bugle and "lights out," as usual. After about an hour of fitfully turning in the August humidity, however, the cadet recruits of each company were abruptly awakened and hustled into formation in front of their company letter on the dark barracks quadrangle. The freshmen stood rigidly at attention in the dark, waiting. Then, the cadre leaders of each company, which included corporals, sergeants, and officers, upperclassmen from each class, slow-marched into view. At a synchronized moment across the entire Corps, floodlights simultaneously snapped on in each barracks as the cadre surged forward into the freshmen ranks. A howling session of physical training began along with the implementation of the "brace." The brace is a semi-contorted position of especially rigid attention that would be the assumed position of a freshman or "knob" for the rest of the school year. It was strictly enforced whenever in a formation or in the presence of an upperclassman. After this "Hell Night," which officially kicked off the Fourth Class system, a knob's life consisted each day of inspections, more drills, and physical training.

The Fourth Class system was unrelenting, even at meal time. Each day, knobs were summoned to formation in the barracks by bugles, then marched to The Citadel's mess hall. The entire Corps of Cadets took their lunch and dinner together in a regimented, semi-formal meal. Additionally, knobs were required to report to early morning formation and marched to breakfast each day. At The Citadel's mess hall, during the three daily mandatory "family style" meals, the freshmen were assigned in pairs to sit at a table along with five upperclassmen. At the table, or "mess," each knob sat on the edge of his seat, "bracing" throughout the meal, working in tandem with his classmate to serve food, keep glasses full, answer trivia questions from the upperclassmen, and — in between, when given permission — attempt to eat. All of this was done while bracing and with the prescribed motion of "square meals," the cadet recruits bringing their forks up vertically, then straight to their mouths. The daily regimentation, the intense scrutiny and corrections, and the unrelenting discipline forced every knob to dig down and find a way to either persevere or quit. Before the end of the nine months, many took the latter path. But those who remained absorbed the traditions of the Corps that originated in 1842. Throughout this process it was the upper class cadre's job to push and weld us together with our fellow classmates, often brutally challenging us to succeed. While there was no love lost for the members of the cadre, we did hold them in grudging respect as we knew they had endured everything they were putting us through.

Late August brought a new level of pressure as regular classes began and academic rigors were added to a cadet recruit's burden. But this new phase also brought relief as quiet study times were mandated in the barracks and the cadre's reach did not extend into the academic halls. These shifting windows of respite and intensity, between academic and military challenges, required a cadet recruit to manage his time and balance the competing requirements for survival. At their core, the academic rigors combined with the Fourth Class system produced stress. How an individual cadet handles this stress – managing priorities, finding a way to persevere and lead those around him through the storm – is the hallmark of The Citadel.

I endured the nine months of "knob year" in the Fourth Class system and, for the most part, passed my academic classes. At the end of that year, I stood proudly in the ranks with my classmates after "Recognition Day," the formal and final rite of passage from the Fourth Class system to becoming upperclassmen. One of the last aspects of "recognition" for knobs was a day of reckoning with the cadre when we held a company beach party and knobs were allowed to "call out" and challenge any of the upperclassmen to a wrestling match in the sand. This traditional reckoning at the end of each knob year served to curb excessive hazing and was also a lesson for all involved that you must be prepared to stand up and account for what you believe in and for your actions. By the end of knob year, I had come to completely embrace every aspect and tradition of the Corps at The Citadel.

After completing knob year in May 1986, I returned that summer to Fort Benning and the Infantry School to complete my training as an infantryman. Meanwhile, the U.S. Army was in the midst of a massive rebuilding effort under President Ronald Reagan. Standards were raised and the Army had plenty of resources and funding. As the training commenced, we were given numerous challenges to test and build us into infantrymen. Advanced Infantry Training consisted of more exercises in the field among the pine forests and red clay ridgelines of Georgia. Our instructors taught us individual skills and drilled us in small-unit tactics. We were broken down first into four-man fire teams, then combined into squads and, eventually, platoons. We fired hundreds of rounds through our M16A2 rifles and used numerous other types of weapons, from grenades to anti-tank rockets. We did all of this while assaulting trench lines and digging defensive fighting positions in the hard red Georgia clay. During our infantry training, we spent a short amount of time learning to drive and fight from armored vehicles. We formed our armored personnel carriers into small convoys and rolled through endless pine forests, occasionally breaking out into the sandy grasslands of former cotton fields on Fort Benning. However, the greatest emphasis of our training remained on mastering the skills of "light" infantry. This meant walking and patrolling on foot for miles through the Georgia pinelands and swampy river bottoms. After one particularly grueling day, we made a fast-paced march on the back roads of Fort Benning, traversing 17 miles through the July heat. As evening finally approached, we followed our drill sergeants off the paved roads and turned down a rough pathway into the forest. Darkness fell as we continued to walk, stopping only to receive brief instructions from the drill sergeant, who warned us to follow closely as they led us along the trails. Soon, we began to enter trench lines and defensive positions that grew deeper and more extensive. Suddenly, from our left flank, machine-gun tracer fire tore through the air, seeming to crack right above our heads. Instantly, the drill sergeant ordered us up and over the side of the trench to our left, into the direction of the fire. While we knew it was not actually combat, it was incredibly intimidating, and our reactions relied upon discipline and conditioning to immediately obey and go over the top. The tracer fire continued to rip overhead and explosive simulators were set off around us as we low crawled our way through the famous "night infiltration course" at Fort Benning. This was just one of a long series of intense and realistic training events that characterized the Army Infantry School in the 1980s. After another hot Georgia summer and eight more weeks of intense training, I graduated from Infantry School and returned to Charleston and The Citadel in August.

I reported back to Charleston and The Citadel early and prior to the rest of the Corps. I returned not only as a sophomore upperclassman, but also as a cadet corporal. I had returned early as I had been selected to be part of the training cadre of C Company, now preparing to receive the incoming class of 1990 knobs. I would remain on cadre, in successively higher positions, for the next three years I spent at The Citadel. Eventually, in my senior year, I was selected to be a cadet lieutenant and the cadre platoon leader, responsible for training freshmen knobs in C Company.

In those days at The Citadel, upperclassmen were still subjected to the same regimentation and basic military discipline, even after completing knob year. But for upperclassmen, life was considerably less intense and more congenial. The quality of a Citadel upperclassman's life increased with each passing semester as he was awarded various "privileges," such as weekend passes or the ability to cut across the parade deck on the way to class. While no longer subjected to the Fourth Class system, upperclassmen continued to adhere to the regimentation, inspections, and military discipline of the Corps. By the end of their four years at The Citadel, many cadets had grown weary of the drill, the uniforms, and the unrelenting regimentation of life in the Corps. Others, like me and many of my fellow cadets, reveled in it all and our hearts rose to the skirl of Scottish pipes and heavy drum beats as we shouldered our rifles, marched in parade, or strapped on our swords for duty with the Corps. Along with the pride I felt in being part of the Corps, I also loved living in the city of Charleston.

The city of Charleston was the ideal setting for a military school like The Citadel. One of the oldest and most historic cities in the country, Charleston moved forward slowly in the 20th century. In those days, Charleston honored its history while hosting The Citadel, providing an old-world backdrop filled with style and grace.

Besides the routine of cadet life and duties with the cadre training the knobs, I majored in history, went to class, and studied in The Citadel's academic halls under veteran military officers and former Ivy League professors. One of my instructors was a grizzled former German officer from World War II. Herr Gundel, a chain smoker, told stories of Panzer divisions between lectures in German class. Another World War II veteran was Lyon G. Tyler, a retired U.S. Navy commander turned history professor. Like so many other aspects of The Citadel, Professor Tyler was a living link to the past. We were astonished to learn that he was the son of a Confederate officer and grandson of U.S. President John Tyler. Professor Tyler's family spanned almost 200 years of American history in just three generations.

Another towering figure in our world was the assistant commandant, Lieutenant Colonel Harvey Dick, who epitomized the great officers who led us during those years. An enlisted Marine during World War II, Lieutenant Colonel Dick then attended The Citadel and graduated to become a U.S. Army officer, serving in the Korean and Vietnam wars. As the assistant commandant of The Citadel during my four years there, he was in charge of discipline and was the most familiar, and possibly most feared, presence on campus. Lieutenant Colonel Dick's attentions were like those of a stern, but idolized, father to the cadets in the Corps.

In addition to the constant discipline, admonitions, and inspiration of the leadership, The Citadel provided constant reminders of the sacred and spiritual importance of duty and military service. One of the most iconic of these reminders is Summerall Chapel in the center of the campus. Located opposite the four barracks that housed the Corps of Cadets and looking immediately across the parade ground, the white structure of stone and glass embodied not only religious ideals but the spiritual essence of The Citadel. Everything about the building reflected the majesty of God and the sanctity of serving and defending our nation. On that building, reverence is written in stone and brass, with the name of each Citadel graduate killed in war-time service enshrined in the chapel. The duality of the building's spiritual themes reaches its peak in the huge marble plaque, centered above the altar in the chapel apse, which reads:

To the Glory of God and in Memory of The Citadel's Patriot Dead

Immersed in this atmosphere and completely committed to these beliefs, I dedicated myself to all the ideals I was learning. To that point in my life, no single place captured the importance of patriotically serving and the clarity of my military calling like Summerall Chapel.

Along with shining shoes and brass, and white glove inspections, I continued to train. I met Army Rangers face-to-face for the first time in Reserve Officers Training Corps (ROTC) class. They were at The Citadel teaching Army cadets in the ROTC department, attached here from the 1st Ranger Battalion stationed in nearby Savannah, Georgia. These sergeants brought with them the uncompromising standards of the 75th Ranger Regiment. They stalked

44

around The Citadel in stiffly starched olive drab jungle
fatigues and black berets, professional, all business, and
above the rest. They were Rangers like Mike Hall and
Rick Knight, veterans of the invasion of Grenada, on loan
from the Army 1st Ranger Battalion in Savannah just an
hour south of Charleston. I had tasted the Army at Fort
Benning but, from these professional warriors, I began to
learn lessons of stone and steel, of absolute discipline and
combat focus at all times. Falling out of a run or quitting
when it gets tough are surrender. Take any mission and
give 100 percent. Train every day to go to war. I learned
everything I could from the Rangers and the other military
instructors, while simultaneously immersing myself in the
duties and traditions of The Citadel. One lesson I failed to
learn in those days was that of balance.

Along with ROTC training, my cadet duties, and
academic studies at The Citadel, I was also still serving as
an enlisted infantry soldier in the Army National Guard.
Prior to reporting to The Citadel that summer of 1985,
I had transferred from the New York Army National
Guard to South Carolina and joined a mechanized infantry
company in Charleston, located just outside the gates of
The Citadel. Our unit was equipped with Vietnam-era
M113 armored personnel carriers which we rode, packed in
the rear as we careened around the red clay trails of nearby
Fort Stewart, Georgia.

I attended drill and training one weekend a month, fitted
in between weekend parades, and an array of Corps duties

to include formal inspection and frequent training exercises with The Citadel's Army ROTC detachment. I wanted to do everything possible to train as a soldier at The Citadel and in the Army, but to my 20-year-old mind, academics was a sideshow. I narrowly believed my studies were just a stepping stone to being commissioned into the Army.

With that attitude, I plowed through each semester, reveling in my history courses but struggling with math and science. Nevertheless, as soon as each academic year ended at The Citadel, I packed my gear and marched off to spend all summer in the Army, just as I had done at the end of knob year. These summers saw me at Fort Benning for Advanced Infantry Training, then at Airborne School after my sophomore year, and finally at ROTC summer camp at Fort Bragg, North Carolina, just before my senior year at The Citadel. Within days of completing these U.S. Army courses each summer, I would rush back and report early to The Citadel. Arriving weeks before most of the Corps, I joined the cadre each year to welcome and train the new class of knobs. Between the Army and The Citadel, the cycle of training seemed endless.

Finally, in the summer of 1989, I graduated from The Citadel. Under oak trees draped in Spanish moss in front of Bond Hall and the monument to the Citadel's Confederate dead, I was handed my diploma by one of The Citadel's greatest presidents, Major General James A. Grimsley. Grimsley was a member of The Citadel class of 1942 and an infantry combat veteran of World War II who had led infantrymen again in Vietnam. He was keenly perceptive and had a deep understanding of the importance of institutions like The Citadel and its traditions. Having seen the "sharp end" of combat, he understood that war could be brutal and harsh, and it required leaders with characters of steel to bring their soldiers through the fires of combat to survive and to win. Not only did he clearly understand the importance of the Fourth Class or knob system, he had the prescient understanding that its unique aspects were largely misunderstood by the civilian world. Demonstrating the character and resolve idealized at The Citadel, Major General Grimsley skillfully resisted the efforts of the outside world, which was—even at that time—trying to recast The Citadel in a kinder and gentler mode. Ingeniously, he proactively invited the media to come and cover the school, effectively setting the stage for the Corps of Cadets to tell its own story. Sadly, he was the last of his kind, being followed by a succession of bureaucrats in uniform, without combat experience or a real understanding of the purpose of the Fourth Class system. They have allowed the school and its traditions to atrophy and rot, genuflecting to political correctness and groveling for personal praise and recognition.

In 1989, however, I was proud to stand on the stage at the south end of the parade ground and graduate with a degree in history. Immediately after receiving our diplomas, all of the seniors going into the Army quickly returned one last time to our barracks rooms and changed from the formal cadet uniforms of gray and gold into Army greens.

In the Citadel Field House, next to the ROTC building named for an alumnus and one of my Confederate heroes, Micah Jenkins, I was formally commissioned as a second lieutenant in the Regular Army. As my family pinned the gold lieutenant's bars on my uniform and the short commissioning ceremony ended, so did my time at The Citadel. Like most of my classmates, I left feeling absolutely dedicated and resolute about serving my country. I also knew that I had been forged by the traditions of The Citadel and, during the previous four years, had taken on every challenge possible to prepare myself for whatever lay ahead.

Prior to graduation that spring, I got my first taste of Army bureaucracy as we completed the administrative process to become officers and get our assignment orders. Earlier that year, we had filled out forms to request which branch or job we wanted to enter. Though the forms had spaces for us to list ten choices to be ranked in the order of our preference, I only filled in one with "infantry." When our branches were posted that spring, to my shock and dismay I was assigned to the field artillery, a branch I had not requested. Further, it seemed an unlikely match given my recent struggles with math. I protested, using "the chain" up through the senior Army leadership of ROTC at The Citadel, but to no avail. I would follow my orders and march off that summer to the U.S. Army's Artillery School in Oklahoma.

2

Climbing the Mountain

A pint of sweat saves a gallon of blood.
General George S. Patton, War as I Knew It

I reported in that summer of 1989 to the U.S. Army Field Artillery School at Fort Sill, Oklahoma less than a month after pinning on my second lieutenant bars and graduating from The Citadel with a degree in history. The artillery is an old and honored branch in the Army that turned out to be a great experience. However, it was still not going to be my place. Fort Sill is a dusty old Army post, spread across the rolling hills and plains where Geronimo and his band of Apache had once ridden. Now, those vast spaces are covered with artillery firing ranges and oil wells. At Fort Sill, U.S. Army artillerymen are routinely joined in training courses by their U.S. Marine counterparts and many foreign allies. Just as Fort Benning is ground zero for the infantry, Fort Sill is the epicenter of field artillery and firepower. Its practitioners commune there in a world of art and science, of physics and ballistics mixed with rules of thumb and fire for effect. At Fort Sill, we studied the ancient calculus of gunnery: prop weight, meteorological data, and the effects of the curvature of the earth. We learned on antique slide rules, side by side with state-of-the-art computers. Along with the classroom equations and faculty of fire directors, I found a small minority among the artillerymen called "fire supporters." They were like outcasts from the scientific chorus of logarithms and gunnery equations. Fire supporters went forward with the infantry to direct and control the artillery fires. In the chaos and maelstrom of battle, they were often the lifeline for the infantry, connecting them to all the devastation the artillery could bring. Fighting with the infantry and other combat arms in the front line of battle, fire supporters or "forward observers" (FOs), as the artillery soldiers were formally called, used the vast array of weapons systems from across the military to engage the enemy. The FOs moved as part of the infantry units, carrying not only the ruck and the rifle, but also heavy radios as their link to the big guns and aircraft. Among the fire supporters at Fort Sill, I also met more Rangers. They were pure fire supporters, not artillerymen sent down to the infantry and banished from their parent units with divided loyalties. These Ranger FOs were assigned to the 75th Ranger Regiment and lived by its creed. Until I could get through the maze of Army bureaucracy and back to the infantry, my immediate goal was to be a fire supporter in a Ranger battalion. To do that as an officer, my first step would be to go to the U.S. Army Ranger School.

Ranger School is a fabled and enduring institution with a legendary status. That legend was built on grueling difficulty and invaluable training. Each year at The Citadel, a handful of cadets competed, through tough training run by the Army Rangers in ROTC, for the privilege of attending Ranger School during the summer. Upon their successful return, they told stories of grueling patrols in the swamps and mountains with little food or sleep. As a Citadel cadet, I was unable to compete for a slot at Ranger School due to the fact I had to focus more on passing my math and science requirements than military training in order to graduate.

Conceptually, Ranger School is designed to teach leadership through the process of conducting infantry patrols in all kinds of environments and conditions. In the heat and cold, mountains, deserts, and swamps, Rangers must not only endure and perform individually, but also lead their fellow Rangers to successfully complete a variety of missions. Ranger School begins with a couple initial weeks of graded assessments and selection exercises to include exhausting physical training and obstacle courses. Weeks of nonstop, relentless training follow, pushing each Ranger to his limits before he can graduate and wear the coveted "Ranger" tab on the shoulder of his uniform.

During my artillery training course at Fort Sill, I volunteered and began the initial training to compete for a Ranger School slot. This initial training consisted of intense additional physical training in the morning and weekly road marches with heavy rucksacks. In the fall of 1989, while still at Fort Sill, I was informed that I had earned one of the Ranger School slots given to our class.

After completing my training courses at Fort Sill, I graduated from the Artillery School and packed up my gear to return to Fort Benning for Ranger School in November. When I arrived, I was met not by the blast furnace I had come to know as a Georgia summer, but by the cool of late fall and the foreboding approach of winter. My "pre-Ranger" training with the Ranger cadre at Fort Sill had prepared me for the various challenges and physical tests. These included the attrition runs and obstacle courses that constitute the first phase of Ranger School at Fort Benning. If a Ranger student fell back more than two paces during attrition runs or failed to complete the obstacle course under the time standards, he was dropped from the course. After the Benning Phase, those that remained moved to nearby Camp Darby. Densely wooded, with forests broken by creek bottoms and swamps, Camp Darby is located in a remote corner of Fort Benning. It was named for a hero of the Ranger Regiment and founder of the Rangers during World War II – Brigadier General William O. Darby. At Camp Darby, we began the long foot patrols and constant cycle of Ranger missions that ran on for days, keeping us tired and hungry. We carried weapons, blank ammunition, heavy packs, and scant food through the waning heat of the days and into the cold nights of Georgia in November. The grueling patrols at Camp Darby, preceded by the first weeks of physical training, constituted the Benning Phase of Ranger School. Though the Benning Phase was primarily designed to cut the class size down by attrition, I made the grade on the first patrols at Camp Darby and successfully continued on to the next phases of Ranger School, in the mountains north of Atlanta and frigid swamps of Florida.

Not only are Ranger students pushed physically, through forest and mountain marches, but they are constantly on edge, being assessed and graded around the clock by their Ranger instructors (RIs). The RIs are veteran Rangers whose job is to teach military skills and constantly monitor students for weakness or failure to maintain standards. During each phase of the course, Ranger students rotate through the jobs of leading patrols and raids, with each position carefully assessed and graded. A Ranger student must not only make it physically to the end of the phase but must pass the RIs' formal grading and assessment in order to proceed further on in the course. Additionally, the Ranger student must make the grade in the eyes of his fellow students. This test comes in the form of a peer-evaluation survey ranking each student in the group, with the bottom 10 percent being cut at the end each phase. This becomes a lottery, with the pool growing smaller as time goes on, a reality that keeps the Ranger student constantly on edge.

The Ranger instructors were professional, tough, and unrelenting. But as former students themselves, they were also occasionally sympathetic. The infantry is a brotherhood and this is especially true among Rangers.

The Ranger instructors knew well the cold nights, exhaustion, and painful long marches of the patrols. One night toward the end of the Darby Phase, as we lay on the cold ground pulling security and facing out among the pine trees, one Ranger instructor quietly walked the perimeter. As he moved among the exhausted men, he bent down to give each one of us a Snickers bar as he celebrated his last patrol as an instructor before moving on to a new assignment. After almost two weeks of little food, almost solely consisting of Army field rations or MREs (Meals Ready-to-Eat), this was a significant boost. To this day, I have a special place in my heart for Snickers bars.

Our greatest test during the Ranger course came after we left the Mountain Phase in northern Georgia and moved south in mid-December to the swamps of Florida at Eglin Air Force Base. By the time we arrived, winter had begun in earnest. Instead of tropical beach weather, the Florida panhandle gave us frigid swamps, soaking rain, and near-freezing conditions. That December of 1989, while patrolling the swamps and pinelands, we could hear around us in the adjacent training areas and on the airfields a great rumbling mass of aircraft and units. Isolated in our world of constant training missions, we were unaware that the U.S. military and the 75th Ranger Regiment were assembling and training for the invasion of Panama in order to take down its dictator, Manuel Noriega. The Ranger Regiment was currently rehearsing its role in the impending operation there in Florida, and it would be just a week before the actual invasion would take place. But I, and the Ranger students around me, remained oblivious to the growing storm. Cold, wet, and hungry, plodding through the swamps, we were merely trying to survive our patrols. This was one of the ultimate tests we would face as unseasonable weather brought snow and ice to Florida and the wet swamps pulled the heat from our bodies. Numerous students went down with hypothermia and mild frostbite as the RIs carefully herded us through the swamps to high ground, checking their watches and using U.S. Navy cold water exposure charts. Our Ranger class passed through these cold and troubled waters with only minor injuries, but four years later, another class would not be so lucky.

In the December class of 1993, four Ranger students died from hypothermia as the RIs struggled to evacuate them from the waters of the deep swamps. One of them was my friend, Milton Palmer, whom I knew from The Citadel. Milton was the top-ranking cadet in the class of 1990, a year behind me, and he was one of the best officers I knew in the Army. As a lieutenant, Milton had been taken out of an earlier Ranger School class with a cold weather injury of hypothermia. A few years later, in the fall of 1993, after we graduated from the Infantry Officer Advanced Course, he went back to Ranger School, keeping his previous injury a secret in order to get a second shot at a Ranger tab. Milton was tragically overcome by the cold and his life cut short in the Florida swamps. To this day, I think of Milton when fall comes and the weather begins to cool and my fingers and toes begin to ache.

Our Ranger School class was a "Christmas Class" and, having successfully completed the Florida Phase, we returned to Fort Benning a few days before the holiday. After the Florida Phase, we were given a short break to recover at home with family before returning for the last phase and completion of Ranger School. We returned to Fort Benning from Florida on December 20, my 23rd birthday, and I celebrated with my favorite Army ration, a tuna MRE, as we offloaded the U.S. Air Force planes at Lawson Army Airfield. Later, as we stood outside in formation, the commander of the Ranger School, an older Ranger veteran named Colonel Keith Nightingale, addressed the class and announced the news about the invasion of Panama. Earlier that morning, the United States had invaded the Central American nation with the entire 75th Ranger Regiment spearheading the operation with a "forced entry" airborne assault. Our Ranger School class included a number of "Batt boys," young privates assigned to the Ranger battalions. When we were released for the holiday later that day, many of them rushed back to the airfield to find space on U.S. Air Force transport flights bringing resupply and reinforcements down to Panama. Once on the ground there, they successfully linked back up with their companies. Although they had missed the initial invasion and combat parachute jump, they did manage to spend a few days in the combat zone before being sent back to the U.S., arriving just in time to report to Fort Benning for the last phase of Ranger School.

The Ranger students from our class who had made it through the Florida swamps continued on to the last phase of Ranger School after returning from the Christmas break. This final test, known as the Desert Phase, was conducted in Dugway, Utah. In early January, after flying from Fort Benning and parachuting into the high mountain deserts of Utah, we conducted our patrols amid the deep drifts of Rocky Mountain snow. Huddled around our Yukon stoves in Army tents, we planned our missions, then walked miles through the desert on our final graded events. But after the wet, bone-chilling swamps of Florida, the desert patrols seemed easy and we practically cruised to graduation. After "tabbing out" in Utah, meeting all the requirements to graduate, we flew back to Fort Benning for Ranger School graduation. At the simple ceremony held on one of the outdoor training fields on Fort Benning, we pinned the black and gold Ranger tab on the right shoulder of our uniforms. I was now a Ranger or, at least, a Ranger School graduate. I had completed a major step in both my career and in my journey toward serving in the 75th Ranger Regiment.

Before applying to the 75th Ranger Regiment, however, new officers – even graduates of Ranger School – are required to prove themselves on a tour of duty with the Regular Army. Before leaving Fort Sill the previous summer, I had secured orders to the 2nd Infantry Division in South Korea and I prepared to leave the United States in the early weeks of 1991. In the late '80s and early '90s, before the decades of war in the Middle East that were to come, Korea was one of the most intense or "high-speed" assignments available. The U.S. Army was still heavily committed to Europe, but the threat of the Soviet Union had begun to wane. I had always wanted to go to Europe, and initially, while still in the Artillery School at Fort Sill, I had gotten orders for Germany. However, the bureaucracy of the Army assigned me to a Lance missile battalion, about as far from the infantry as you could get. Lance missile units were like a military version of NASA. Interesting, but far afield from the infantry where I wanted to be. So, I began a long personal tradition of working the system and making appeals, especially to fellow Citadel graduates, to get a different assignment. While still at Fort Sill, before going to Ranger School, I got an opportunity to change my orders from Lance missiles in Germany to the 2nd Infantry Division, forward along the Demilitarized Zone (DMZ) in South Korea. With its aggressive communist enemy, Korea was one of the top choices at that time for those seeking to prove themselves, as I was.

After graduating Ranger School, I arrived in Korea in February 1990. I served a few short months on the staff at an artillery battalion then was sent down to join the infantry. While diving deep into the Asian culture and humping the steep mountains and rice paddies, I served as the fire support officer (FSO) for an infantry company in the 1st Battalion,

503rd Infantry. The 503rd Infantry Regiment had a rich unit history. Being airborne paratroopers in World War II, they had made one of the most daring parachute assaults in history onto the Japanese-held island of Corregidor in the Philippines in 1944. The combat parachute assault was made even more dangerous by the extremely limited size of the tiny polo field used for the drop zone, surrounded as it was on two sides by cliffs over the ocean. Incredibly, the 503rd was able to get most of its men landed on the polo field and then overcome the stunned Japanese defenders. In that assault, however, many of the paratroopers were shot out of the sky while coming down and a few missed the polo field, dropping down the surrounding cliffs and into the ocean. This proud and aggressive tradition was carried on in Korea as the 503rd, now a "light infantry" battalion, lined up with the rest of the 2nd Infantry Division and our Korean allies to stand against the communist North.

U.S. Army "light" battalions were infantry units which had few vehicles and fewer heavy weapons. Their focus was on tough training, individual infantry skills, and rapid deployment. Our battalion of approximately 500 infantrymen was part of two brigades of American soldiers assigned to the 2nd Infantry Division. The 2nd Infantry Division had been permanently stationed in South Korea since the end of the war there in the 1950s. It stood alongside the South Koreans facing the communist North Korean Army, the fourth largest army in the world with over a million soldiers. The American contribution to the defense of South Korea numbered only in the thousands in opposition to this vast communist foe, but it was more than token support. One of the American brigades was composed of M1 tanks and other armored vehicles, providing a mobile strike force to counter-attack and at least blunt any communist offensive across the border. In the eventuality of a war, our light brigade of infantry would infiltrate and hold fast in remote mountain positions, or be flown by helicopter to make air assaults against supply lines and other rear areas. This strategy was designed to allow the defense of South Korea to hold out long enough for American reinforcements to arrive and turn back the red tide.

As light infantry, our battalion would most likely be required to fight in isolation and without much support, relying on tenacious defensive tactics in the tough Korean terrain and leaning on our ability to strike hard and fast against the North Korean rear area. To this end, we maintained the highest degree of readiness, building the skills of our units with constant training and numerous live fire exercises.

As we trained hard, enduring monsoon floods and sweating through the hot Korean summer, we carefully watched the communist horde just across the border. Meanwhile, other events were occurring in the world that summer that also drew our attention and that would change the course of history.

In the Middle East that August of 1990, Saddam Hussein invaded Kuwait, brutally occupying the neighboring country and threatening the Gulf States and Saudi Arabia. U.S. President George H.W. Bush responded, building a coalition to confront the Iraqis with a massive military buildup from the United States and its allies. The military effort, designated Operation *Desert Shield*, assembled in Saudi Arabia and faced the Iraqi Army through that summer and fall. From our defensive positions along the DMZ dividing North from South Korea, we watched as more and more military units were sent to the Middle East. As the military deployment grew in scope, it became so large that even the National Guard began to mobilize. Desperate to get involved with the first war of our generation, I felt trapped in Korea.

As Operation *Desert Shield* continued and days and weeks went by, the end of my one-year tour in Korea approached. Because of the immense requirements of *Desert Shield* and in order to maintain its other defensive commitments globally, the Army had enacted a bureaucratic policy that no troops would move from Korea while the Middle East buildup took place. However, as I closely watched events in the Middle East, I worked the phone back to the personnel division of the Army. After confirming that my replacement, another second lieutenant, was in fact on his way to Korea, I then secured an open slot in the 82nd Airborne Division, which had been one of the first units to deploy to the Middle East that summer. Against the odds, I secured approval to leave Korea, one of the only soldiers to do so during that time. In early February, I prepared to depart from Korea and move to Fort Bragg, North Carolina, before heading overseas to join the 82nd already in position in Kuwait.

The day before I was to leave the 1/503rd's camp near the DMZ and head down to the airport in Seoul, there was an early morning knock at my door. The duty sergeant had brought a message from the headquarters that I was to immediately call my assignment officer at the Department of the Army in Washington, D.C. I quickly moved down to the headquarters below our barracks and got on a secure telephone. As the phone rang in Washington, a captain in the personnel division answered. During a brief conversation, he informed me I was being offered a slot with the 3rd Battalion, 75th Ranger Regiment, at Fort Benning. If I accepted, they would change my orders immediately, cancelling the assignment to the 82nd and deployment to the impending war in the Middle East. He also gave me the telephone number to the S1 personnel officer at the 75th Ranger Regiment headquarters. I promptly called the Ranger Regiment S1 personnel office, reaching a captain on the staff who confirmed I had been selected for the Rangers but gave few additional details. Months before, during the summer, I had attended the 75th Ranger Regiment's recruiting meeting in Korea. I had interviewed with a staff captain and filled out my application, volunteering for an assignment to a Ranger battalion. While I had been closely tracking events in the Middle East and pushing my efforts to deploy with the 82nd, I had heard nothing from the Rangers and nearly forgotten my application. Now, I was at a crossroads. Would I take the orders I had in hand and go to war with the 82nd or follow my original dream and join a Ranger battalion? Convinced none of this was happening by chance and bolstered by my belief that there could not be a war without the Rangers, the Army's spearhead combat unit, I accepted the assignment to the 3rd Battalion, 75th Ranger Regiment.

I spent the next few hours updating my plans and waiting on the new orders to arrive via fax from Washington. My immediate plans, however, did not change as I headed to Seoul and took a commercial airliner back to the United States. I landed in Rochester to spend some leave with my family, where I found everyone was understandably tense and anxious with the war getting ready to kick off overseas. After just a few days at home, I continued on to my rendezvous with the Ranger Regiment in Georgia.

3

Steel Sharpens Steel

Recognizing that I volunteered as a Ranger,
fully knowing the hazards of my chosen profession . . .
1st Stanza of the Ranger Creed

After travelling home from Korea for just a few days'
leave with my family in Rochester, I once again arrived
at the gates of Fort Benning. Landing at the airport in
Georgia, I saw a number of soldiers along the way with
Ranger Battalion scrolls sewn on their bags and with their
distinctive, partially shaved heads or the "high-and-tight"
haircut required by the 75th Ranger Regiment. They
were mostly brooding, standoffish, and palpably focused.
Events in the Middle East began to rapidly culminate, with
the air war against Iraq having begun just weeks before
in January. The sergeants I encountered from the Ranger
Regiment did not engage me closely, as it was one thing
to have orders to the Ranger Regiment, and another to
pass the screening course and be formally accepted into
a battalion. I reported in for the two-week screening
and assessment course, or Ranger Orientation Program

(ROP), with a handful of other lieutenants from various parts of the Army. We spent the next two weeks with the training cadre from the Ranger Regiment there at Fort Benning, passing the physical tests, reviewing basic skills, and learning the history of the 75th Ranger Regiment. Unlike Ranger School, there was no yelling or recruit treatment. We were all officers and this was a "gentleman's course." That said, we were introduced to the stone-chiseled standards of the 75th Ranger Regiment. Failure to meet those standards, be it making the required time on a 5-mile run or safely handling a weapon, would mean immediate and irrevocable expulsion. To be accepted into a Ranger unit, all of these various physical tests and skills had to be checked and passed by every Ranger from the youngest private to the colonel commanding the regiment.

After successfully completing all of the challenges and graded events during our two-week ROP course, our last block of instruction was on how to prepare and wear the distinctive black berets, worn only by the Ranger Regiment. Like everything else in the Ranger Regiment, our berets were historic symbols. They were an immense source of pride and had to be worn uniformly and precisely. Similarly, we proudly sewed on our "3rd Ranger Battalion" scroll patch that went on the left shoulder of our uniforms, just beneath and crowned by our Ranger tabs.

Leaders, such as officers and sergeants, could not serve in the Ranger Regiment unless they had graduated from Ranger School. Junior soldiers (privates through specialists), arrived in Ranger units shortly after their basic training and a short Ranger Indoctrination Program (RIP). Serving in the line in infantry platoons, these young Rangers had to undergo a Laconic spartan system of their own. In line platoons, new Ranger privates were "raised" by their "tabbed" Ranger leaders under intense training and scrutiny until they themselves were able to go to Ranger School. Upon completion of Ranger School, they returned to their units and, having proved themselves, then received a promotion to non-commissioned officer (sergeant) and began to lead other Rangers.

Ranger School is usually the pinnacle of training and the greatest test in the career of anyone who attends and successfully completes it. Most graduates complete the course and move on in their careers to much easier and more normal training environments with Regular Army units. Rarely will they ever again experience anything that approximates the nonstop cycle of intense planning and preparation for missions, followed by airborne parachute or helicopter assaults and long marches through deserts, forests or mountains. Every mission in Ranger School comes with the extreme challenge of mentally and physically putting everything into a raid or combat patrol, followed by immediate reset and starting again. While the rigor and intensity of the training provide a unique experience for most Ranger School students from the Regular Army, this is, in fact, the way of life for an Army Ranger in the 75th Ranger Regiment. More importantly, Army Rangers of the

75th Ranger Regiment live by the tenets spelled out in the Ranger Creed and devote to it every part of themselves, every minute of the day.

Recognizing that I volunteered as a Ranger, fully knowing the hazards of my chosen profession, I will always endeavor to uphold the prestige, honor, and high esprit de corps of my Ranger Regiment.

Acknowledging the fact that a Ranger is a more elite soldier, who arrives at the cutting edge of battle by land, sea, or air, I accept the fact that as a Ranger, my country expects me to move further, faster, and fight harder than any other soldier.

Never shall I fail my comrades. I will always keep myself mentally alert, physically strong, and morally straight, and I will shoulder more than my share of the task, whatever it may be, one hundred percent and then some.

Gallantly will I show the world that I am a specially selected and well trained soldier. My courtesy to superior officers, neatness of dress, and care of equipment shall set the example for others to follow.

Energetically will I meet the enemies of my country. I shall defeat them on the field of battle for I am better trained and will fight with all my might. Surrender is not a Ranger word. I will never leave a fallen comrade to fall into the hands of the enemy and under no circumstances will I ever embarrass my country.

Readily will I display the intestinal fortitude required to fight on to the Ranger objective and complete the mission, though I be the lone survivor.

RANGERS LEAD THE WAY!*

The Ranger Creed is recited as a group within units of the 75th Ranger Regiment at almost every opportunity. Standing together in ranks before major events, from workouts on the physical training field to standing up, packed in the back of a darkened and deafening military aircraft before a parachute assault, Rangers loudly recite the creed together, like a Spartan paean. The Ranger Creed not only extolls you to succeed, but is also a reminder that you have to renew and revalidate yourself constantly, meeting every new challenge. To do otherwise would be to risk failure, letting down your nation, and worse, the Rangers to your left and right.

The Ranger Regiment's history dates back to before the birth of the United States itself as Ranger units fought to protect the colonies. In modern times, the current Ranger battalions also trace their beginnings to their parent units of World War II under Colonel William O. Darby. The 3rd Battalion was newer than the first two, having been organized in 1984 shortly after the success of the original two Ranger battalions during the invasion of Grenada known as Operation *Urgent Fury* in 1983.

* Source: https://www.army.mil/values/ranger.html

During that operation, the 1st and 2nd Ranger Battalions conducted a parachute assault in the early morning hours, jumping from an altitude of just over 400 feet, onto a runway defended by Cuban and Grenadian communist soldiers. The assault was conducted with the two Army Ranger battalions receiving less than 24 hours' prior notice before being assembled and launched toward their objective. After beating down the island's defenses and securing the airfield, the Rangers moved on to rescue 400 American medical students stranded on the island and secured lasting fame in the history of the U.S. Army. I now found 3rd Ranger Battalion to be full of veterans like the Grenada Raiders, the Ranger sergeants I had met back at The Citadel. These combat veterans served in many of the key positions, from battalion senior officers down to the infantry platoons and squads. The modern 3rd Ranger Battalion had also been "blooded" during the invasion of Panama, just over a year earlier in December 1989. During Operation *Just Cause*, all three Ranger battalions and the regimental headquarters mounted parachute assaults to spearhead the U.S. invasion of that Central American country. The 3rd Battalion was a mixture of its own proud heritage and the standards and proven performance of the veteran Rangers from the other two battalions.

Following graduation from the Ranger Orientation Program, after receiving our black berets and reciting the Ranger Creed, two other lieutenants assigned to the 3rd

Battalion and I departed the headquarters compound of the 75th Ranger Regiment. We immediately headed to report in to our new assignment, walking the short distance through a maze of brown, screened security fences, to the headquarters of the 3rd Battalion nearby on Fort Benning. The 3rd Battalion shared space "next to the flagpole" on Fort Benning with the 75th Regimental Headquarters, while its two sister battalions (1st and 2nd) were stationed at Hunter Army Airfield in Georgia and Fort Lewis, Washington, respectively.

Reporting in to the Battalion S1 or personnel officer, we were given a brief but sincere welcome. He was expecting us and quickly informed us of our new assignments. I would go to Alpha Company to be the fire support officer (artillery). In this job, I would work closely with the Alpha Company commander Captain Craig Nixon, a quiet, stoic officer who had been wounded during the Panama invasion. Nixon had only a few more months to go in command when I arrived in the early spring of 1991. My time with Craig was brief, involving just a handful of training missions there at Fort Benning before he changed command. Further curtailing our time together, I would soon depart, going on temporary duty (TDY) to a wide variety of military schools and training courses to learn a host of new skills I would need as a Ranger fire support officer. In spite of the short time Craig Nixon and I had working as a team, we developed mutual trust and became good friends. Although he left 3rd Battalion that summer, changing out of command and departing for Korea, I would soon see him again.

Over the next few days, as I transitioned from the selection and screening course at ROP and moved next door to my assignment at 3rd Ranger Battalion, the ground war in Iraq began. Soon after we arrived in the battalion, the two other new lieutenants and I were in-briefed on what was happening with the war and the role the 75th Ranger Regiment was to play. It seemed one reinforced company of about 140 Rangers from the 1st Ranger Battalion in Savannah had been deployed to Kuwait and was now conducting small raids against Iraqi targets. It was further revealed that in the months prior to the opening of the war, 3rd Battalion had been assigned the mission of supporting a special operations task force whose job would be to rescue Americans detained by the Iraqis at the U.S. embassy in Kuwait.

Alpha Company had been training for this mission previously on Fort Benning when a horrific nighttime bus crash killed one Ranger sergeant and critically injured the Ranger fire support officer who preceded me. Captain Nixon, the company commander, dove to the floor of the bus as he saw the head-on collision coming, and escaped death once again as he had done in Panama. It would not be the last time.

The injury of the Alpha Company fire support officer and requirement for an immediate replacement was the reason for my selection and last-minute notification in

Korea. However, shortly after the bus crash occurred, Saddam Hussein ordered the release of the American hostages in Kuwait and the rescue mission was scrapped. These shifting events now put 3rd Battalion at the back of the line for deployment to the war. With the end of combat in Iraq coming just a matter of hours after the invasion began, the remainder of the 75th Ranger Regiment never got out of the gate and remained home in the United States.

We spent the next few months watching the returning soldiers of the Regular Army strut around Fort Benning, brashly pointing to their combat laurels and asking us, "Where were you?" We knew this was a one-off for the Regular Army and that, at some point, the 911 call would come in again and the fire bell would ring for us. Meanwhile, the Rangers returned to the cycle of week-in and week-out training like we were going to the Super Bowl.

After our in-briefs and formal welcome to the battalion, I went down to Alpha Company. It was manned not only with many veterans of Grenada, but most of the Rangers were recent veterans of Panama as well. For the Grenada veterans, Panama had been their second combat parachute assault and they carried two gold stars or "mustard stains" on the Airborne wings of their uniforms. Some of the older veterans had been with 1st Ranger Battalion back in 1980 and seized an airfield in Iran during Operation *Eagle Claw*, as the Rangers assisted Delta in the Iran hostage rescue attempt. When I arrived at 3rd Ranger Battalion in 1991 there was no lack of combat-experienced veterans, just as at any period in its history.

Among the group of iconic soldiers who led Ranger units in those days, none was more legendary than the regimental sergeant major Mariano Leon-Guerrero ("LG"). The regimental sergeant major is the senior enlisted soldier in the 75th Ranger Regiment and is its standard bearer, a modern-day centurion. Sergeant Major LG was known to every Ranger in the regiment not only because he was the absolute epitome of what a Ranger should look and act like but because he was constantly out in the field with the Rangers at training events. On numerous occasions I would climb into the back of a helicopter and find myself packed in next to Sergeant Major LG. One of the greatest stories the Ranger veterans of Operation *Just Cause* told me was of the flight into Panama as the 75th Ranger Regiment prepared to make the parachute assault which would spearhead the US invasion. The 75th Regimental Headquarters personnel had been cross-loaded and were flying aboard the same aircraft as Alpha Company. Aboard the blacked-out aircraft, just minutes before the doors opened to begin the jump, Sergeant Major LG stood up and climbed on top of a pallet of ammunition. His voice boomed above the noise of the aircraft engines as he led the densely packed Rangers in reciting the Ranger Creed and reminding them of their duty.

Sergeant Major LG often seemed to gravitate to my fire support team during training. On one occasion during an exercise on Fort Benning he explained that during the Vietnam War, as a young enlisted soldier, he had actually been a forward observer before later switching to the infantry. He went on to relate that on one patrol in Vietnam his lieutenant had been killed fighting alongside him. He gave me a serious look and said, "A lot of them got killed – the fire support officer has a dangerous job." As was his Pacific islander tradition, he then placed the back of my hand on his forehead before moving off to see more training.

In spite of my time as an enlisted private in the Army National Guard and my year in Korea with the Regular Army, I felt woefully inexperienced among these veteran Rangers. Arriving in Alpha Company, I learned that, although I had previously served as a fire support officer in Korea, this job would require different skills. Rather than rely on standard artillery, the Rangers primarily used aircraft, helicopters, and their own light mortars for support. Calling in fast-moving fighter jets, special operations aircraft like the AC-130 gunship, and special operations attack helicopters would take extensive additional training. Fortunately, I was sent off almost immediately to a number of excellent schools to learn these new skills. I spent weeks with the U.S. Air Force, Navy, and Marine Corps, learning to call for naval gunfire from ships and other skills such as bringing in close air support from military jet aircraft or "fast movers," as we called them.

One of my favorite missions at that time with the Rangers was to be on the ground with a team carrying laser designators and radio beacons. These small teams of Rangers would penetrate behind enemy lines and guide U.S. aircraft onto critical targets with their radar beacons, then point them out with their lasers to enable precision attack. Today, military aircraft carry their own laser and have GPS (global positioning system) navigation or work with unmanned aerial vehicles (UAVs). But in those days the ground lasing team was one of the most "high-speed" missions that Ranger fire support teams trained for.

After The Citadel and the isolation of Korea, life in Columbus, Georgia – the city just outside of Fort Benning – seemed plush. For the first time since high school, I began to experience some normal aspects of a social life. When we had time off, life was good, but there was not much of it. Occasionally, for a change from the military town atmosphere of Columbus with its hordes of trainees and soldiers, I drove an hour to Atlanta and went out on the town with my best friend from high school Mike Jennings, now a mechanic with the airlines there.

While officers in a Ranger battalion are not treated like Ranger School students, the cycle and intensity of training was largely the same. Each of the three Ranger companies (Alpha, Bravo, and Charlie) within the battalion trained largely on an individual cycle. Each company of roughly 150 men was composed of three rifle platoons and one weapons platoon. Rifle platoons were further divided into squads of Rangers carrying small arms like the M4 rifle, Squad Automatic Weapon (SAW) as well as light machine guns (M240s). The weapons platoon provided the greatest punch within the company, normally attaching teams of snipers and anti-tank weapons teams to the rifle platoons. The weapons platoon also had a section of two 60mm mortars to provide indirect fire support. The mortar section worked closely with my team of Ranger forward observers. My team consisted of six FOs, my team sergeant, and me. For missions, we attached two-man teams of FOs to each rifle platoon to assist them in engaging and calling for fire support. My job during Ranger missions was to stay with the Ranger company commander, usually just behind or alongside the rifle platoons, coordinating on the radio with the various fire support assets that were a part of any given mission. Ideally, but not always, I would pass these assets, like the AC-130 or AH-6 helicopters, over to my FOs, the "end users" in the rifle platoons.

Ranger companies received missions passed down from our immediate higher headquarters at 3rd Battalion and, likewise, above that from superiors higher up in the chain of command, at the 75th Ranger Regiment and so on, up to the Joint Special Operations Command (JSOC). Sometimes, these missions would call for a single Ranger company to deploy, while others required the entire Ranger battalion to deploy for training in different parts of the world and usually arriving directly by parachute assault.

When not conducting training with the other Ranger or special operations units, Alpha Company worked in the field, training and practicing the myriad skills that every

Ranger is required to master. Each year, we spent months training on weapons, parachute and helicopter assaults, raids (especially on airfields), and long "movements to contact," looking for the enemy in the hardest terrain we could find. We knew that conducting missions in jungles, swamps, and mountains under harsh conditions – similar to Ranger School – would keep us prepared for actual combat. The training was continuous and there could never be much real downtime; if a sudden threat to the United States arose and lives were at stake, the response would need to be immediate. Faster than ships can sail, and certainly faster than any ponderous and extended military buildup would take. With no prior notice, a Ranger unit had to assemble, load aircraft, and be in the air headed for a crisis spot anywhere in the world in a matter of hours, such as they had done in Grenada. The unit had to be prepared and sharp, with gaps immediately filled with replacements. This level of readiness required constant, intense training. This was the case for every member of a Ranger battalion and especially for the Ranger FOs of a fire support team, known as a FIST. Ranger FOs had the dual responsibility to maintain their place alongside the Rangers in the infantry rifle platoons while simultaneously remaining current on their complex fire support skills.

As I returned to Alpha Company in the late summer of 1991, after my weeks of "school house" training, our team began to rotate out some of the senior sergeants who had been in position since Panama. Fortunately, the Rangers who were moving up to replace them in the leadership positions were also Panama veterans. These men who had been with the company during the invasion of Panama as young privates were now becoming leaders and were some of the best soldiers I have ever served with. The new FO sergeants – Jerry Straight, Brian Smith, and Mark Pellerin – were all not only veterans of Panama but, as young privates, had been raised in 3rd Battalion under its intense, and sometimes harsh, training. My new team sergeant, Mark Hartley, was an experienced, cerebral soldier who had previously served in the 82nd Airborne Division before transferring into the Rangers. All of these veterans took me in, along with a batch of new Ranger privates who arrived on the team around the same time. Immediately, we began the process of welding together a skilled and cohesive team through various training exercises over the coming months.

As I had come directly from my assignment in Korea, I was still a second lieutenant when I arrived at 3rd Ranger Battalion. This was an advantage in the long run as it gave me time to serve over three years with the Rangers. Most lieutenants only average about a year before they are promoted and have to move on. During that time, I was able to not only attend numerous military schools and courses, but also participate in all of the standard recurring exercises for the Ranger Regiment.

In Alpha Company, I also worked intensely on the individual skills required to be a Ranger and leader, such as becoming a master parachutist. To become a master parachutist, a Ranger must "exit the aircraft" and complete 65 military parachute jumps. He is also required to have graduated from the intense U.S. Army Jumpmaster School. At Jumpmaster School, students learn a number of critical skills, such as the art of physically inspecting and rigging parachutes and equipment onto soldiers to prepare them for a jump. The jumpmaster also learns how to lead and control the actions of the group, or "chalk," of paratroopers inside the aircraft during the flight as they prepare to jump. This includes the incredible experience of opening the jump door at the rear of the airplane and hanging outside in the "prop blast" to observe and confirm the plane is on the proper approach to the drop zone. After a Ranger leader has mastered all of these skills, personally jumped 65 times, and been formally in charge of a number of parachute operations, he is awarded a new set of silver Airborne wings with a jumpmaster wreath above the parachute. During my time serving in Alpha Company, I successfully completed all the requirements, except for the total number of jumps needed. A few years later, I would officially become a master parachutist while serving as captain on my second tour with the Ranger Regiment.

In addition to individual training, we also worked intensively on our team's fire support and basic job skills. Our team pushed the envelope, traveling all over the country to train with various fire support assets like the

U.S. Air Force AC-130s based out of Florida and Army helicopter gunships of the 160th SOAR from Kentucky. Combined with the training exercises we participated in as part of Alpha Company, we were kept in the field or out on the range with little break.

In 1992, Colonel Dave Grange, Jr. took over as commander of the 75th Ranger Regiment and a fast-paced training cycle became even more intense. Colonel Grange was the son of one of the Army's legendary generals. Colonel Grange's father, Lieutenant General Dave Grange, Sr., was an infantry officer and three-war U.S. Army veteran who cast a long shadow. His son, Dave Grange, Jr., was intensely competitive and strove to equal, if not outdo, his father's legacy. By 1992, he was well on his way, having served as a recon platoon leader with the 82nd Airborne in Vietnam, then becoming a Special Forces officer (Green Beret) and, later, an Army helicopter pilot. Dave Grange, Jr. had a career path not even possible in today's Army, one that represents quite an accomplishment. As a captain, Dave Grange, Jr., commanded the company from 1st Ranger Battalion that had gone into Iran in 1980 as part of Operation *Eagle Claw*. He next tried out for the Army's elite and secretive Special Forces Operational Detachment–Delta and was selected to serve as one of its senior officers. An experienced veteran, Iron Man triathlete, and inspiring leader, there were few men who could equal Colonel Grange's reputation or drive. As the 75th Ranger Regiment commander, Colonel Grange made it clear that chief among his priorities was to get the Ranger battalions into action and take on America's enemies.

With the recent collapse of the Soviet Union, these enemies now ranged from Saddam Hussein, battered but still defiant after *Desert Storm*, to communists in North Korea and South America. There was also the faint, but continuous, hum of Middle Eastern terrorists, like wasps circling and threatening to sting. We tried to keep up with the news, to glean any window of opportunity that might require Rangers to spearhead action, but most of our attention soon became focused on the fast-moving train Dave Grange was bringing.

Under Colonel Grange, the nonstop training of the Ranger Regiment reached a new level of intensity. Bringing the regiment out from behind the black curtain of special operations, we were now "guns for hire," so to speak, for any major military command in the world that had a potential combat mission. Along with the requirement to keep our individual and team combat skills at a razor's edge, as well as our primary commitment to U.S. Army Special Operations "black" missions, Grange put us into every theater of the world where a crisis might develop. The Rangers' arrival there was almost always by forced entry. Most military units deployed on a schedule, as part of a gradual military buildup, landing at a secure airbase, boarding buses or trucks, then moving to barracks before assembling for operations. This was a luxury we did not enjoy in the 75th Ranger Regiment and rapid deployment

was one of our preeminent skills. Colonel Grange wanted
to showcase for the entire world that, with little or no
notice, Rangers could deploy anywhere on the globe and go
immediately into combat while taking on the most difficult
missions. In the Ranger battalions under Colonel Grange,
our world became flying from our home bases loaded onto
sleek U.S. Air Force C-141 transports. With their long
noses and high-arching tails, C-141s very appropriately
resembled Viking longships. Packed into these warships, we
flew shoulder-to-shoulder with our weapons and combat
gear stacked on top of us, then violently parachuted out
into training missions all over the world.

A parachute assault with the 75th Ranger Regiment
is more intense and different than anywhere else in the
Army. Needing all the combat power they can get, as many
Rangers as possible would be packed tightly into the back
of the aircraft. These aircraft could be the long, narrow
C-141 cargo jets or smaller, propeller-driven C-130
"props." The C-130s were usually from the U.S. Air Force
but were occasionally aircraft flown by our allies. Every
weapon, piece of equipment or type of supplies we would
need was either packed and carried by the Rangers or
pushed out the back of the aircraft with us. With main and
reserve parachutes, weapons, ammo, rucksack, radios, and
other gear, every Ranger staggered to get inside the aircraft
carrying hundreds of pounds of weight. On long flights,
we would carefully "rig," putting on our parachutes while
packed into the aircraft, praying not to tangle a line or

strap, which might inhibit and collapse the deployment of the parachute. As the aircraft approached the drop zone, they flew in a tight formation while the Rangers in back rose in darkness under dim red lights and the bellowing orders of the jumpmaster. After staggering to our feet under the backbreaking weight of our equipment and shuffling forward toward the rear doors, Rangers pressed in with helmets pushed into the pack of the men in front of them. Once I had become a more experienced paratrooper, I would always tell the Ranger behind me to give me "a few steps" for space as we went out the door in order to keep some distance and a safe spread in the air to help avoid a collision. Once in formation, the Air Force transport aircraft would buck and weave, buffeted by their neighbor's jet wash as they attempted to slow to "drop speed" while maintaining their tight "stack" formation. Inside the aircraft, it was often like a rollercoaster in a blacked-out tunnel, packed against the men in front and behind, hunched over and straining against the weight, the jets and airstream blasting in our ears. Next came the thundering noise when the jump doors slid open. In those final tense minutes, all eyes attempted to glimpse the glowing red light beside the door. When the pilots believed they had navigated to the initial point and were over the drop zone, they switched the door lights to green and the Rangers launched forward like a spring. The compressed chalk of Rangers would aggressively surge toward the door or out the lowered tailgate ramp, streaming into the thunder of the prop blast, and relief from the backbreaking weight. On these jumps, the goal was to fling yourself out the door and keep your body rigid until that prop blast hit you like a wave. As you hurtled away from the aircraft, the rush of the parachute deploying was followed by an easy descent and a few hundred feet of momentary peace. At the same time, you constantly scanned the air to avoid colliding with other Rangers and risk collapsing your parachute canopy or his. Checking below us, we would release our heavy rucksacks, which had been strapped across the front of our legs by the jumpmasters. The heavy packs would drop to float below us, like an anchor still tethered by a long nylon line.

As we descended down into the unknown, we would remain mentally fixated on whatever target our unit had been designated to hit. After a few tranquil seconds floating in the air, the landing was often bone-jarring. If uninjured, this was followed by rapidly getting our weapon out of its case and ready for action, then weaving through the spider's web that had been the parachute and its lines. FOs had the additional task of immediately getting their radio into operation and making communications checks before packing away and stowing the parachute. Within minutes of hitting the ground, every Ranger was required to be racing toward a designated assembly area, often navigating at night over rough terrain to join the rest of the company. Within minutes of landing and assembling, the Ranger company would move off to begin the attack on whatever target they had been given.

Led by Colonel Grange and our legendary sergeant major, Leo Guerrero, the 75th Ranger Regiment conducted these "forced-entry" parachute assaults around the world, from Korea to Kuwait, Twentynine Palms to Thailand, and numerous places in between. Sometimes the flights were more than 12 hours long but they always culminated in the blacked-out, thundering chaos of a Ranger forced-entry operation. The parachute assaults would then be immediately followed by moving into a live fire training exercise.

In addition to our rapid deployment and forced-entry expertise, the hallmark of the 75th Ranger Regiment was to push the limit to train as close to combat conditions as we could during peacetime. We conducted all of our missions with real ammunition, or "live fire," as the Army referred to it, which included the array of fire support called in by my team of forward observers. We took on every asset and integrated anyone who could meet our high training standards, bringing in fast-mover jet fighters, artillery, naval gunfire, and – as always – our own light mortars and special operations aircraft, like the AC-130 gunship and AH-6 special operations helicopters.

Deploying around the globe, we trained with the British Parachute Regiment in Scotland, the Commandos in Belgium, and the U.S. Marine Corps in Nevada. Nearly always arriving by parachute assault, we then conducted long, arduous foot marches which would lead to a live fire attack across places like the Scottish moors or western deserts in the U.S. After each mission, we would immediately reorganize, clean our weapons, and get a few hours' rest before loading aircraft to return to base to begin planning the next mission. This intense, tumultuous pace went on for months and brought the Ranger Regiment to a level even its veterans had not imagined. But, it came with a price.

Invariably, during intense, realistic training, there are accidents. In the swirling dust of Nevada that fall, B Company lost Ranger sergeant Jeffrey Palmer, who was accidentally shot when he crossed into the fire of other Rangers. During a training mission in October 1992, as our battalion provided support for 1st Ranger Battalion, which was training for continued missions in Iraq, we suffered another major loss.

While Rangers normally deploy from their home bases in the United States to foreign theaters, by the forced-entry parachute assault, once there they often depend on helicopters for mobility. Like many other things, these rotary-wing special operations are performed differently than in the Regular Army. No "pax" seats or seat belts, but packed in with weapons and gear, the outboard Rangers tied in, seated on the edge of the doorway, legs dangling out. Mounted aboard the aircraft of the 160th SOAR, Rangers can move swiftly from their parachute drop zone or any "postage stamp" landing area, flying hundreds of miles to strike targets and raid an enemy's position. Best of all for Ranger FOs, these special operations aircraft carry a devastating array of weapons, bringing immense firepower to support Rangers on the ground. While missions occasionally called for Rangers to stealthily walk in and assault targets, some of our greatest capabilities were demonstrated when we mounted the helicopters of the 160th "Night Stalkers."

This was the type of mission being rehearsed that October in 1992 as 1st Ranger Battalion trained to strike targets in Iraq. The remote and mountainous deserts of Dugway, Utah replicated northern Iraq. A Ranger company was given the mission of conducting a rotary-wing raid on a simulated "Iraqi objective." Third Ranger Battalion would support the exercise. I was deployed, along with about 30 other Rangers from Alpha Company, to Utah for the training event. Our job was to spend days role-playing as Iraqi soldiers in the simulated camp. That was the only thing being simulated, however. The training mission for a Ranger company from 1st Battalion would be a live fire, and the Ranger force would come in aboard the Blackhawks, flying low through the mountains by night, over a long route that included passing over the Great Salt Lake. On the night of the exercise, as the formation of Blackhawk helicopters skimmed above the lake, they passed over a narrow causeway. The trail aircraft of this formation was a USAF special operations helicopter containing a number of key leaders, to include the USAF squadron commander and the commander of 1st Ranger Battalion, Lieutenant Colonel Ken Stauss. With Stauss in the helicopter was my commander from 3rd Ranger Battalion, John Kenneally, there to observe and provide feedback. Bringing up the rear of the tight formation, flying under night vision goggles, the USAF pilots could not discern the causeway and struck it at over 100mph, causing their aircraft to crash into the lake and killing most of the U.S. servicemen on board. Miraculously, one of the USAF pilots survived the crash, floating in the lake until he was rescued by legendary Ranger medic "Doc" Donovan. Donovan had been monitoring the exercise at a nearby Air Force base, waiting for the live fire to begin. But upon learning of the crash, he rushed to the water's edge. Seeing the burning aircraft about a mile out, he commandeered a tiny rubber boat and paddled through the darkness and frigid waters to the wreck in time to save the struggling pilot.

Lieutenant Colonel John Kenneally had been not only a commander but a mentor to many of the junior officers, and his loss was a hard one. These were not the only losses suffered in training by the Ranger Regiment that year. More Rangers were killed that year during intense training than most units lost in combat during *Desert Storm*.

During our downtime that summer of 1992, amid the intense and frenetic pace of training and life in a Ranger company, I had managed to meet a beautiful girl who worked at a local Columbus restaurant outside of Fort Benning. Beth was from an old Columbus family and worked part-time at the restaurant while going to college. By the fall of that year, Beth and I had been dating just a few months, most of which time I was deployed. The night of the helicopter crash, Beth was at work and saw on the news that "Rangers had been killed while training in Utah." Knowing I was with the Rangers out in Dugway, she waited for days to hear if I was safe, until finally I was able to call back to Georgia. The anxious tension of not knowing and not being able to get any information was a hard introduction for her to the facts of life in the Ranger Regiment.

Despite the occasional losses and injuries, the intense pace of training for the Ranger Regiment continued under Colonel Grange. As 3rd Battalion prepared to depart for the annual "Team Spirit" exercise in Korea,* I proposed marriage to Beth on a cold night in early March and she accepted. Elated, I flew out of Fort Benning the next night with the rest of the battalion on a 19-hour flight to Pusan (now Busan), South Korea, where we conducted a forced-entry parachute assault onto the frozen rice fields.

The Rangers spent the next few weeks conducting raids on targets such as headquarters and other critical posts all over South Korea. Between raids, while dug in on a frozen hilltop position, our company was inspected by a U.S. Marine Corps three-star lieutenant general who told us we were "the most disciplined unit" he had ever seen. He could barely believe we had flown nonstop from the U.S., parachuted into Korea, and had been continuously

---

* TEAM SPIRIT was an annual combined joint exercise conducted in the Republic of Korea that included all the various US and Korean military services.

conducting raids ever since. As the exercise came to a close, we had a few hours off before leaving Korea. I took a short pass and went into the village outside the U.S. base. Heading straight to one of the local Korean tailors, I bought an "Army mess dress" uniform. The Army mess dress is like a military tuxedo and a cut above the standard blue dress uniform that officers wore. I would wear it just a few months later at the chapel on Fort Benning when Beth and I were married in June 1993.

Because of the intense training routine, leave – or vacation time off for Rangers – was scheduled as a group, or "block," so that the entire unit, one battalion of the Ranger Regiment at a time, would simultaneously take leave for two weeks. This occurred twice a year for each battalion, and time off outside of these two scheduled periods was rarely permitted. During these block leave periods, weddings for Rangers and girls from Columbus would often occur back-to-back in the chapel on Fort Benning. During the June block leave in 1993, Beth and I were married there at 1600 hours, and another Ranger officer and friend of mine, Captain Jim Klingaman, married his bride Kathy at 1800 hours. Jim was a dry-witted and brilliant officer, then working in the operations section (S3) of the battalion staff. We would continue to serve closely together in the coming months.

In addition to marrying a beautiful girl from Georgia, joining Beth's family brought me in touch with their extensive history in America and the South. They were related to George Washington and their family story dated back to the first colonists in Virginia. I was especially interested to read about Beth's ancestor, Major John Thomas Carson, who had commanded the 12th Georgia Infantry, a Confederate regiment raised in central Georgia during the War Between the States. John Carson had enlisted as a private when the war began but he was soon elected to be a junior officer. He and the 12th Georgia served in every major battle with Robert E. Lee and the Army of Northern Virginia, usually at the center of the fighting. Carson was promoted numerous times and eventually became a major and the senior officer in his regiment. After being captured at Spotsylvania, Virginia in 1864, he was returned in a prisoner exchange just a few weeks later. After all he had endured, Major Carson still took only a few days' leave at home in Georgia before returning to Virginia. Weeks later, he was killed at the head of his regiment in the Shenandoah Valley. As I traced the path these Georgians blazed through battles like Antietam/Sharpsburg, Chancellorsville, and Gettysburg, I was amazed at the courage and fortitude the soldiers showed time after time in some of the heaviest combat Americans had ever witnessed. Their example, standing fast against all odds, became a deep inspiration for me. I would carry their memory with me as a standard through all the various battles of my career.

After Beth and I got back from our honeymoon and block leave was over, Alpha Company returned to training. Every year, my team of FOs would travel to Fort

Campbell, Kentucky for an exercise called "Gunsmoke," where we focused on working with the attack helicopters from the 160th along with other special operations fire support assets like the USAF AC-130 gunship. We spent days and nights on the ranges at Fort Campbell, bringing rocket and machine-gun fire as close and accurately around our positions as possible. The raw power of the Gatling guns and rockets of the AH-6 helicopters, tearing up the ground within meters of our location, is unequalled in fire support. We knew that of all the assets that supported us, these pilots and their gunships were both our main shield and sword.

The pilots of the 160th are simply the finest in the world. They have thousands of flying hours, many more than Regular U.S. Army pilots, and they have special expertise using night vision goggles. They are also absolutely dedicated to mission accomplishment and often just as aggressive as Rangers in their pursuit of targets. If anyone trained as much or more than the Ranger Regiment, it was the 160th SOAR. Not only did they have to keep their flying skills at an absolute peak, they also had to support both the training and real missions of all the various U.S. Army Special Operations forces, from the 75th Ranger Regiment to the SFOD-D "black," or most secretive, elite units. This kind of dedication required not only incredibly skilled pilots, but warriors.

The annual "Gunsmoke" exercise was a chance to not only work with the pilots of the 160th but get to know them and develop a common understanding and bonds of trust. During this "Gunsmoke," I again worked closely with Chief Mike Durant, a Blackhawk pilot I had teamed up with on a number of previous exercises. Mike was quiet and patient, never getting excited and always finding a way to make the mission happen in spite of obstacles. Mike was also a combat veteran, having flown with the 160th during the Panama invasion and *Desert Storm*. Like the rest of the Night Stalker pilots, he exuded a cool confidence and we had no qualms flying anywhere with him. We knew that, no matter what happened, if we were on the ground Mike Durant and the other pilots of the 160th would be overhead providing fire support and would never stop until they could get us out. Working with units such as the 160th and many others in the U.S. Special Operations Command gave us not only great pride but also great confidence.

We also knew the 75th Ranger Regiment had the best soldiers anywhere, and we proved that every time we deployed around the world. We had the best training as well as the full weight of the U.S. military, the only global superpower, at our disposal. The U.S. military had proven over recent decades that it had no peer and the Ranger Regiment was its spearhead. The only level above the Rangers were the operators of Delta, many of whom came from the Ranger Regiment and whom we supported and fought alongside on black missions. These missions were directed by the highest levels of the government and were usually highly complex and dangerous as well as being critical to the national interest. They were given the highest priority and support by the U.S. government and nothing was spared. When the Ranger companies conducted black combat missions with Delta, we thought ourselves almost invincible. The Ranger leaders knew that this confidence and skill was due largely to our training and constant drive to get better. Part of these efforts to improve included studying military history. As a college history major, I naturally gravitated to this.

During that summer of 1993, a book titled *We Were Soldiers Once and Young* came out, describing one of the first large battles of the Vietnam War in the Ia Drang Valley in 1965. Co-narrated by Joe Galloway, a journalist who was present at the battle, and Lieutenant Colonel (later Lieutenant General) Hal Moore, battalion commander of one of the key units, the book was like a combination of *The Iliad* and an Army tactics manual. In 1993, Moore was living in retirement near Columbus. That summer, he was invited to a meeting of the officers of the 3rd Battalion to talk about the book and his experiences. He brought along his battalion sergeant major from the battle, Basil Plumley, who was also retired and living in Columbus. Basil Plumley was an iconic three-war paratrooper who had made combat parachute jumps in World War II and Korea before fighting in Vietnam.

In 1965, Moore and Plumley led the 1st Battalion of the 7th Cavalry, formerly Custer's infamous command. Moore was the master for us junior officers and he sagely compared the fight in the Ia Drang with Custer's disaster at Little Big Horn. The parallels were eerie. Moore had taken his battalion of close to 500 men looking for the enemy deep into the valleys of the Central Highlands of Vietnam. "Air Cavalry" – not riding horses, but mounted in UH-1 light helicopters – the 1st Battalion, 7th Cavalry confidently flew deep into territory prowled by an undetected North Vietnamese Army (NVA) infantry division. Moore's men landed in the Ia Drang and, once on the ground, moved forward while the sound of the departing helicopters receded in the distance. Soon, Moore's troopers captured two lone NVA lookouts who, like ghosts, echoed Custer's Crow scouts 90 years before, telling him there were "thousands of enemy ahead who wanted to kill Americans." But unlike at Little Big Horn, the 1st Battalion, 7th Cavalry prevailed in the Ia Drang. Moore outlined the reasons for us, which included lessons learned on battlefields in World War II and Korea. Top among these lessons were leadership under fire, keeping a reserve, and, most important for me, U.S. firepower. The battalion officers listened carefully to these and many other lessons Moore and Plumley tried to pass on, but we still could not completely relate. The U.S. military had come a long way since Vietnam. It was 1993 and we were part of a military that had space-age technology and unparalleled intelligence assets. We believed our leaders would never commit us to an untenable situation. We might have to fight but, because the U.S. had no military peer, we could not comprehend the overwhelming odds and desperate struggle faced by this cavalry battalion almost 30 years earlier. I held the utmost respect, akin to awe, for these veterans and their story, but I could not imagine myself ever having to face a similar test of arms.

Just a few weeks later that summer, after Beth and I had been married a couple of months, she called me at the company headquarters. I could tell by her voice something was up and she quickly got to the point. She had been to the doctor that day and he confirmed she was expecting a baby. I was used to the fast-paced life of a Ranger but, in just a few weeks, I had been married and was now going to be a father. Additionally, I had recently received orders to attend the Infantry Officers Advanced Course there at Fort Benning to begin in September. When Ranger officers are promoted, they are required to leave the unit and go back to the Regular Army, doing a tour in a job at their newly achieved rank before they can reapply for assignment to the Ranger Regiment. By 1993, I had been a lieutenant for over four years and would soon be promoted to captain.

There was another major surprise that summer as I was called to the battalion commander's office one day. The battalion commander doesn't often meet with lieutenants and I entered with an air of apprehension. Jim Klingaman had recently become the adjutant, or S1, for the new commander, Lieutenant Colonel Danny McKnight. Both of the men received me wordlessly in the commander's office, then stiffly handed me an official letter. I had no idea what was going on or what to expect. However, I was soon relieved to read that my long-standing request for a transfer from the artillery to the infantry had finally been approved by the Army headquarters in Washington, D.C. after years of slowly working its way through the staff bureaucracy. The Army almost never allowed a lateral transfer from one combat arm to another, and I had submitted the paperwork over a year prior when John Kenneally had been in command. I had all but forgotten about the request. As I lowered the letter in disbelief, McKnight and Klingaman both broke into big smiles, laughing at my initial concern and congratulating me on the rare outcome.

As I only had a few short months remaining in the battalion, it was decided I would remain in my slot as a fire support officer and close out my time before moving on to the Advanced Course. In the meantime, I was officially transferred on the Army rolls over to the infantry and once again wore the crossed rifles and blue cord, which I had earned years earlier as a private.

All of these surprises and changing events had their impact. I was still in Alpha Company and training continued, but I found my mind wandering to other concerns. I thought about my next career steps and where I, or rather where *we*, should be assigned as I would be bringing a family for the first time.

In addition to all of this, Colonel Grange had completed his assignment with the Rangers. He formally changed command of the Ranger Regiment that summer, passing the reins to another colonel. With his departure, the intense surge of worldwide deployments and training missions abated somewhat. In spite of his efforts, the 75th Ranger Regiment had not been committed to any "real-world" combat missions. In fact, we had watched some Regular Army units deploy, departing for peacekeeping missions, to include relief efforts in the country of Somalia on the Horn of Africa.

The U.S.-led United Nations mission to feed starving refugees in the chaotic, failed state of Somalia had begun with the initial invasion by U.S. troops in December 1992 under the orders of President George H.W. Bush. The mission had achieved initial success, securing the key cities of Kismayo and Baidao and the capital, Mogadishu. Once U.S. troops had become established on the ground, the rival Somali militias faded into the background and the stage was set for the UN to provide humanitarian aid to the starving refugees. In addition to the food and relief supplies, the U.S.-led coalition was able to bring relative stability to some of the major Somali cities. By early February, the initial mission with its objectives of humanitarian relief had been achieved. But by this time, President Bush had left office. Under his successor, Bill Clinton, the mission soon began to change. Pressed by the UN Secretary General for aggressive disarmament of the Somali militias and emboldened by early successes and the relative ease of securing the country, Clinton began to gradually implement a plan for "nation building" to attempt to reestablish a modern civil society in Somalia.

In spite of some initial success, the breakdown of society in Somalia was a complex problem and the country had a troublesome history. At a geographic crossroads between tribal Africa and deep-rooted, expanding waves of Islam, Somalia's population fused many aspects of both of these cultures. One of these factors in Somali culture was a radical element of Islamic Sufism called the Dervishes, which had taken root in Somalia around the turn of the century. The "Whirling Dervishes" were a military-religious organization known for their radicalism and fanatical disregard for death. This was often demonstrated by the young men of the clan militias who recklessly fought each other in the ruined streets of Mogadishu but at this point had largely avoided the UN security forces. However, this soon began to change.

The creeping evolution of the mission in Somalia went on through the spring and summer of 1993. Back at Fort Benning in 3rd Ranger Battalion, we began to hear occasional reports of flareups between the UN forces and the Somali militias. This news smoldered in the background while our training went on and I absorbed all the changes going on in my life.

In the battalion area and around the headquarters, we had picked up loose threads of rumor that a special operations task force may be needed in Mogadishu. But these passing rumors were drowned out by the constant hum of activity in the battalion. They were soon forgotten as I prepared for the coming next steps in my life and Army career, causing me to momentarily take my eye off the ball and for the first time be focused on something other than deploying for war.

In late July, I began the initial process of ordering my affairs, preparing to leave the battalion and to reluctantly hand off my fire support team to another lieutenant being sent to replace me. However, I was excited to begin the Infantry Officers Advanced Course at Benning. At the same time, Beth and her family were also beginning the standard rituals of preparing for the expected arrival, with baby showers and unending shopping that seemed to include more gear than my Ranger fire support team possessed. But before I would depart from the battalion and begin my classes, I had one more duty, one more deployment for training.

In order to be able to immediately respond to a crisis within hours of being called, each of the three battalions of the 75th Ranger Regiment must rotate through a schedule of increased readiness posture. This increased readiness was somewhat like firemen waiting at the station for the bell to ring. This duty status was referred to as the Ranger Ready Force (RRF) and, during this time, the battalion that was on call, or RRF1, must keep all of its Rangers within 30 minutes of base at all times, ready to respond. Equipment was pre-positioned and prepared to move, bags were packed, and the battalion stayed in a heightened state of readiness for a period of about 60 days before the duty was rotated to another battalion.

Third Battalion assumed RRF1 that summer of 1993 and would stay on it through most of August, nearly coinciding with the completion of my tour. RRF1 was often a painful inconvenience, but had become routine as I had been through it many times during my three-year tour in the Ranger Battalion. There was a significant change for this particular RRF1, however. Instead of being tied to Fort Benning, the battalion would deploy to Fort Bliss, deep in south Texas on the Mexican border, for a large-scale exercise in the mountainous deserts. The concept was that the battalion would already be assembled and, if called on to respond to a crisis, could deploy directly from Fort Bliss. This month-long training exercise would include other special operations units and numerous fire support assets. These included, of course, our teammates from the 160th SOAR, and I looked forward to a last round of intensive live fire exercises on the vast desert range complex at Fort Bliss.

At the beginning of August, as I packed my gear for Fort Bliss, Beth and I talked about the baby, my upcoming course in September, and potential next assignments. We said our goodbyes for what we thought would be just a few short weeks as I headed to Fort Benning, reporting to the battalion for my last training exercise.

Within hours, the battalion flew out of Fort Benning and arrived in Texas by parachute assault. When the jump doors of the aircraft opened, the vast brown desert sharply contrasted with the green pinelands we had left in Georgia. For the Rangers, Fort Bliss was an ideal training site. We had numerous ranges, mountains, and miles of broken desert terrain for fire and maneuver. As the training units assembled around the airfield at Fort Bliss, Alpha Company drew the first slot in the training rotation for the company live fire exercise.

This exercise would be heavy on fire support and included U.S. Marine Corps Harrier jets dropping bombs while our mortars suppressed the objective. These would be immediately followed by AH-6 "Little Bird" gunships from the 160th pounding a mock-up target, while the Ranger infantry platoons maneuvered and cleared the site. My fire support team in Alpha Company were experienced Rangers, with the Panama vets having been replaced by a new generation who had honed their skills through numerous training events. Among my lead forward observers were Sergeants Butch Galliete and Wayne Lessner. They both showed their skills during the exercise, bringing the gunship fire in so close that spent brass casings rained down on the assaulting Rangers.

Following the successful live fire exercise, Alpha Company reassembled at the battalion area in a small tent city by the airfield. Each tent held about 20–25 Rangers sleeping on cots but we were glad to have the shelter, along with air conditioning and hot food, or "chow," as the Army called it. As the company of Rangers moved into the area and settled into tents, we began to reorganize and prepare for the next training mission. Not long after our arrival in the battalion area that day, things began to stir. Something was drawing the attention of the headquarters staff and news began to trickle in. Over in Somalia, two American HMMV trucks had been ambushed and four U.S. troops had been killed. Today, that news would barely make the headlines, but in 1993, after decades of relative peace, this was a major event that rippled through the nation. As we sat in our tents and absorbed that news, our company commander came in looking crestfallen. He had just returned from the battalion headquarters where he and the other senior leaders had been briefed on a classified order from Washington, D.C. The company commander somberly began to brief the key leaders gathering on the cots in our company headquarters tent. A special operations task force was being formed at Fort Bragg, North Carolina to deal with the deteriorating situation in Somalia and 3rd Battalion had been ordered to send one Ranger company to join that task force. Our neighbors in Bravo Company had been selected for the mission. That news hit us in Alpha Company with a shock wave of disappointment, but I barely had time to absorb it as a runner arrived with a message from the battalion headquarters. I was being urgently called to report to the battalion commander, Lieutenant Colonel McKnight. Not having time to think about what was going on, I hurried off to the battalion headquarters tent.

4

Drumbeat

Then I heard the voice of the Lord saying, "Whom shall I send?
And who will go for us?" And I said, "Here am I, send me."
Isaiah 6:8

Lieutenant Colonel Danny McKnight greeted me
cordially, but with an air of seriousness, when I arrived at
his tent. As I knocked and walked in, he asked me, "Are
you ready?" When I immediately gave him the standard
Ranger answer, "Hooah, Sir," he quickly got to the point.
McKnight informed me that the lieutenant who was my
fire support counterpart in Bravo Company had departed
Fort Bliss just hours before and gone home for a family
emergency. Bravo Company would be departing to join
the task force now assembling at Fort Bragg in a few hours
and the FSO position had to be covered. The battalion
commander then informed me I would be the replacement.
Third Battalion would also be sending an additional rifle
platoon from Alpha Company and a few other personnel.
When I was told these additional personnel would include
another one of my FO sergeants, I immediately decided

on Butch Galliete. My other veteran FO sergeant, Wayne Lessner, would also be going with 1st Platoon.

There have been a number of times in my life when I felt events were moving beyond my control but with a sublime purpose. A few years before, as I prepared to depart Korea, events had similarly aligned at a critical juncture to bring me to the Ranger Battalion, rather than join the 82nd Airborne during *Desert Storm*. Now, the fractional timing and narrow window of opportunity struck me as beyond coincidence. Winston Churchill had similar thoughts when he said:

The destiny of mankind is not decided by material computation. When great causes are on the move in the world, stirring all men's souls, drawing them from their firesides, casting aside comfort, wealth and the pursuit of happiness in response to impulses at once awe-striking and irresistible, we learn that we are spirits, not animals, and that something is going on in space and time, and beyond space and time, which, whether we like it or not, spells duty.[*]

I have always had a deep faith in the Lord. Raised in a family divided between Roman Catholics and Southern

---

[*] "Birth Throes of a Sublime Resolve," broadcast June 16, 1941, https:// winstonchurchill.hillsdale.edu/man-is-spirit/?utm_source=rss&utm_ medium=rss&utm_campaign=man-is-spirit.

Baptists, I drew from both for spiritual guidance. For most of my life, my Christian beliefs were far stronger than my actions, but I knew the Lord was guiding my path and the events unfolding now were a stunning reminder.

Back in our tents in the Alpha Company area, after briefing Sergeants Galliete and Lessner, I quickly packed my gear and weapons. Our teammates worked to assist us, double checking that we had everything we might need. Just minutes after receiving the orders from Lieutenant Colonel McKnight in the headquarters tent, we were packed and left the disappointed gloom of Alpha Company, transitioning quickly to the humming activity of the Bravo Company area.

The tension and excitement in Bravo Company were palpable as preparations for departure were underway. I checked in with the company commander, Captain Mike Steele, and his first sergeant, Glenn Harris. Captain Steele was a hulking former college football player. He had been a starting lineman at offensive tackle for the University of Georgia when Hershel Walker received the Heisman Trophy and they had won the College National Championship in the 1981 Sugar Bowl. I had only dealt with Mike Steele a couple of times back at Fort Benning when he had been on the battalion staff before he took over command of Bravo Company. He had a reputation for being gruff and stubborn but also for being a completely dedicated Ranger.

Though he had kept his distance from the lieutenants and other junior leaders, I had caught a glimpse into another side of Mike earlier that summer. Mike had used his own unique recipe when he had won a chili cook-off at one of the many social events the officers of the battalion were required to attend. This event was an informal "Hail and Farewell," where new officers were welcomed and those departing for other assignments were recognized. At this particular event, wives were included and Mike had enthusiastically promoted his chili, making sure everyone got a taste. When the judges finally picked his chili as the best, Mike gleefully announced that his secret ingredient was squirrel meat, a revelation that made more than one Ranger wife turn green. Mike's wife, Leigh, was one of the finest ladies and best people I had met in the battalion. Where Mike was intimidating and gruff, Leigh was sweet and charming, full of Southern grace. Mike and Leigh had two young children, both of whom would go on to serve in the Army. Their son, Dane, would later serve as an infantry lieutenant and platoon leader in 3rd Ranger Battalion.

Now, as we entered the B Company tents and I walked over to Captain Steele and First Sergeant Harris, it was all business and intense focus. They cordially welcomed us but there was little time for discussion as the aircraft taking us to Fort Bragg would soon depart. My FO sergeants and I, along with the rest of the Rangers from 1st Platoon, melted into B Company's ranks and began the process of loading the aircraft. Along with the reinforced B Company, the 3rd Battalion commander Lieutenant Colonel McKnight would be coming along to Fort Bragg, as well as a handful of other Rangers and staff who would provide support wherever the task force may need it.

We were all on a fast-moving train now, working to keep up with events and to process what was happening, waiting to see what the mission before us at Fort Bragg would be. As the big U.S. Air Force C-141 jet roared down the runway and lifted off from Biggs Army Airfield, we knew intuitively that the task force would be organized and commanded by the Joint Special Operations Command with Delta as the main player for the mission. We also guessed we were going to Somalia in response to the deteriorating situation there. We talked to other Ranger veterans and got glimpses of previous special operations missions where Ranger units had teamed with Delta. From these accounts, we knew that on previous missions, the Rangers had captured airfields or added troops and combat power to Delta raids. With this in mind, we tried to anticipate what our role might be. However, at that time, missions involving Delta were highly classified and black, with discussion and insights being frowned upon, even among their partner units. Delta operated in the shadows, going in as the spearhead, conducting lightning fast missions during U.S. military operations, or lurking on the fringes, observing foreign wars. Little was seen and less was officially spoken of Delta, even within Special Operations Command. At this point, flying east across the United States and approaching Fort Bragg, we could only speculate.

Landing at Pope Air Force base, adjacent to Fort Bragg in North Carolina, we got off the transport aircraft and loaded onto buses. Instead of heading onto the huge main post complex of Fort Bragg, we drove west toward the remote pinelands. After weeks in the desert, we could smell the forest again, and the farther we drove into it, the more our tense expectancy began to rise. We finally pulled into a secluded and secure base camp, primarily used by special operations forces. There, we unloaded our gear and moved into a small temporary camp made up of the familiar Army green tents, similar to what we had left at Fort Bliss.

A Ranger is used to living out of his rucksack and taking shelter under a rain poncho and he is happy to have dry socks and eat a vacuum-packed military ration Meal, Ready-to-Eat (MRE) out of tinfoil and a plastic bag. Hot food from a mess hall kitchen and a tent to sleep in was comfort for a company of Rangers. Dropping our gear in the tents, the company was soon called to load back aboard the buses bringing our weapons and individual equipment. As we were anxiously looking for answers to our questions and eager to start our deliberate planning, we were summoned out to one of the nearby training ranges.

Arriving at the range, we unloaded the buses and were met by the sight of small groups of Delta operators moving around buildings staged nearby in the trees. As company FSO, responsible for all aspects of fire support, I always stayed with the company commander, to include during the planning and coordination of missions. As Captain

Steele and I walked up to the range, we searched for the Delta leaders. Very brief introductions were made to a few of the leaders standing near us. Then, as the rest of the Rangers unloaded the buses behind us, the Delta leaders asked Captain Steele if we were ready to start. Somewhat taken aback, neither Captain Steele nor I initially grasped what they meant. When we realized that the Delta leaders were proposing to immediately run through an exercise, then and there, on the "mission profiles," or ways we would conduct our mission, we were more than surprised. Captain Steele informed the Delta leaders we had literally just arrived at Fort Bragg and had not even been briefed on what the mission or plan was beyond the vaguest outline, much less made a plan of our own. The Delta leaders seemed frustrated at this answer. They seemed to fail to grasp that, not having been briefed, we lacked almost any insight into what was going on or was required and they were anxious to start working things out.

In the Ranger Regiment, one of the key aspects of our operations was exhaustive and comprehensive planning. In the planning of each mission, we followed a methodical process and sequence, which often seemed pedantic and was usually implemented with excruciating rigor. It was a system that proved its value, however, over and over again in the history of our missions and training. In our planning, little was assumed and all important points were spelled out clearly and briefed down to the most junior private. These briefings were called operations orders. They were the holy writ, spelled out in the Ranger handbooks, used in Ranger School and throughout the Ranger Regiment. The goal of our planning and the operations order was not to have a perfect plan but to ensure every Ranger had a clear picture of what must be accomplished and how the team would accomplish it. While Ranger planning has evolved to more streamlined processes, the baseline approach remains the same. The tension Captain Steele and B Company were experiencing with the Delta leadership was, to some extent, cultural. Not every special operations unit goes to the lengths that Rangers do in planning. Indeed, a rigid system can sometimes be detrimental, so a degree of flexibility is a good thing. But this was beyond different approaches or a clash of cultures. As the lead player, Delta had obviously been working on this mission for some time and they didn't seem to grasp that we were literally walking on at a cold start.

As Captain Steele and I, along with some of the other Ranger key leaders, tried to pull what information we could from the short conversations at the range, most of the Delta operators moved on and began to wrap up their training session. We loaded the buses again and returned to our Ranger camp. Some of the additional Rangers from headquarters were arriving there in the tent site and I saw Jim Klingaman beginning to set up a small staff area. He told me he had come along from Fort Bliss with the battalion commander and would provide any staffing assistance to the mission that he could. My quick conversation with him

revealed he had not been given much information on the
mission yet either, beyond the scraps we already knew. Still
searching for more information, later that day I went with
Captain Steele and some of the other Ranger leaders to the
Delta compound in anticipation of getting a mission brief
and to continue coordinating.

The compound was the military complex that housed
Delta and many of its key training facilities. On the outskirts
of Fort Bragg, it was a semi-independent training and work
center for the operators of Delta. While its proximity to
the main base kept Delta plugged in to all the support that
the huge Army post provided, it allowed them to be largely
autonomous and unencumbered by Army bureaucracy.
Delta and the compound were a special operations soldier's
dream, with glistening new facilities, unlimited resources,
weapons, ammo, and gear. They also had plenty of support
and assistance to take care of the exhaustive administrative
and logistical requirements it takes to keep a military unit
in operation. It was an epicenter of military focus with
one objective: training to achieve the highest skill level of
soldiering possible.

To join Delta, a soldier could apply from any part
of the U.S. Army but had to already be an experienced
NCO or officer. After some initial screening and testing,
an applicant then attended the Delta Selection Course.
Prospective Delta operators who make it through this
grueling selection course have really only taken the first
significant step by earning a slot in the legendary Operator

Training Course (OTC). It is in OTC that good soldiers are forged and honed into the incredibly skilled warriors who must meet the highest standards to graduate and be assigned to an operational Delta squadron.

Like any military organization, Delta was subdivided into subordinate units, beginning with a squadron. It was organized on the British model of the Special Air Service (SAS) squadrons and commanded by a lieutenant colonel. Squadrons were the rough equivalent of a Ranger battalion at the unit level. These squadrons, designated by letters "A," "B," and "C," were arrayed in adjoining wings along the sides of the compound.

Arriving at the compound and checking in through the tight security at the facility gate, we were ushered inside and proceeded to find our way down to the work space of C Squadron, the Delta unit who had been given the mission for Somalia and who we would be partnered with. In C Squadron's small work spaces, we were met by Lieutenant Colonel Gary Harrell, the squadron commander, a burly officer whose rough personality fit well with that of Captain Steele. Also present were a number of other leaders from C Squadron, to include the assault troop commander. He had come to Delta after previously serving in Army Special Forces (Green Berets) which, culturally, has a more laid back approach than the Ranger Regiment. Our welcome to the squadron was cordial, but brief. It was again evident that the Delta leaders had been poring over the mission for weeks and we were coming in at the tail end, trying to catch up. As Lieutenant Colonel Harrell stepped up to a dry erase board, he briefly outlined the mission and their plan.

The National Command Authority (NCA), namely the Commander in Chief President Bill Clinton, had decided to respond to the attacks on UN forces in Somalia and the recent killing of the four American soldiers by directing the formation and deployment of our special operations task force. Its mission was to capture and remove the primary Somali insurgent leader, General Mohamed Farah Aideed, who was operating at that time in the capital city of Mogadishu.

To accomplish this mission, Delta proposed to locate and positively identify Aideed using a variety of U.S. intelligence assets and technology. Once Aideed had been located in a building or vehicle, Delta would fly in and assault the target aboard helicopters from the 160th SOAR, who were even at that moment arriving and being integrated into the task force there at Fort Bragg. Delta's unparalleled skills at clearing buildings and capturing target personnel were especially suited to a quick raid such as this. C Squadron's assault troop was designed to handle the complexities and potential threats of clearing multiple rooms and structures but was not necessarily designed for a stand-up street fight. This is where B Company and its Ranger platoons came into the plan. The Rangers would be needed due to the rapidly deteriorating security situation on the ground in Mogadishu.

At this point, we were also given some background and updates on the situation in Somalia. After the initial success of the invasion in December 1992, the UN efforts in Somalia had changed significantly. The invasion forces, composed mainly of U.S. Army soldiers and Marines, had initially met little resistance and easily secured most of the country. Once this had been achieved, early in 1993, the majority of U.S. forces were withdrawn. The Marines departed earlier in the year and the U.S. Army contingent was reduced as well, being replaced by the forces of other allied countries. As the UN's security situation evolved, General Aideed, leading the Somali National Alliance, began to see an opportunity.

In 1991, General Aideed had been one of the major players involved in bringing down Somalia's last organized government under President Siad Barre. After the fall of Barre's government and in the anarchy that followed, Aideed had been a key leader during the ensuing clan fighting, which had destroyed most of Mogadishu. When the famine in northern Africa caused Mogadishu to be flooded with refugees, the United Nations had tried to respond with humanitarian aid. But the warring militias had hampered initial UN humanitarian efforts, hijacking aid and attacking UN workers. This led the UN to respond with a military invasion led by the United States in December 1992. As the military forces quickly secured the country and relative stability returned, this allowed the UN to successfully alleviate the humanitarian crisis. Later, under U.S. President Bill Clinton, the shift was made to the new mission of nation building.

With the reduction in the U.S. military presence in Somalia and the growing timidity of the UN, Aideed began to resume his efforts to take overall power in Mogadishu. As Aideed harangued his fellow clansmen of the Habr Gidr, his efforts at resistance had increased over the spring and summer. The UN had responded with an increasing number of raids and airstrikes, upping the ante. The growing friction and widening conflict led directly to the ambush focused on U.S. forces and the killing of four Americans, just days before in early August.

As these events began to unravel the efforts of the UN, security in Mogadishu began to destabilize correspondingly. Soon, UN forces were unable to move easily through the streets as Aideed's heavily armed militia had drawn lines around many of the Habr Gidr-controlled neighborhoods in defiance. UN patrols now met resistance moving into these areas or, even more ominously, once in, had to fight their way out against Aideed's rag-tag, but wily and vicious, street fighters.

Capturing Aideed in the overcrowded urban setting among his fellow clansmen would require neutralizing any Somali efforts to assist Aideed around the immediate target area during the raid. The mission to deal with Aideed's militia or mobs in the streets around the target area during Task Force Ranger missions would be the job of the Rangers of B Company.

After giving us the background on the current situation, Gary Harrell continued his briefing on the plan. He described how the teams of Delta operators from C Squadron could potentially assault and capture Aideed anywhere in the city. They would rely on their ability to mount a lightning fast strike from the helicopters, quickly clearing the target to capture Aideed and then withdrawing back to base. The issue was that the relatively small number of Delta operators programmed for the assault would all be needed to clear the immediate buildings or vehicles being targeted. If any nearby Somali militia or clansmen in the neighborhoods tried to interfere or help Aideed during the operation, the assault force would need reinforcement to deal with the additional threat, shielding them from attack and holding back the crowds.

That mission was given to two platoons of Rangers from B Company. To accomplish this mission, these two Ranger platoons would be divided into four groups of about 15 men each. These four groups of Rangers would constitute a security force on the ground with Delta and would establish blocking positions in a solid ring around the target area. Each of the four groups of Rangers would initially be designated as "chalks" and assigned to fly in four MH-60 Blackhawk helicopters provided by the 160th, who would fly them to the target for an assault. The Ranger security force would fly in immediately on the heels of the Delta assault element, who would land at the target first. Once Delta was on the ground, the four helicopters carrying the Ranger chalks would arrive and insert them into predesignated locations at the four corners of a targeted building or area. After the Rangers had fast-roped in and gotten on the ground, the four chalks would establish blocking positions (numbered R1 through R4) and form a tight perimeter surrounding the target building. The blocking positions would have a dual responsibility of keeping any Somalis from interfering with the assault force as well as preventing anyone from escaping the target buildings. If the assault was against a vehicle or convoy, the plan would be similar except that the Ranger blocking positions would be set up on the roads leading into an intersection where a target vehicle might be stopped.

In addition to its speed, we found the beauty of this plan to be its flexibility. To put the entire force of Delta assaulters and the four Ranger blocking positions on the ground would be the "heavy" option. But the size of the force actually committed on the ground could be tailored and reduced to fit the situation. This would depend on the conditions at the target, such as its size, layout, and the number of Somalis involved. Additionally, those decisions could literally be made on the fly, even while the entire force was airborne and en route to the target on board the helicopters. With a few short and simple orders from the commander, Lieutenant Colonel Harrell, aviation commander Lieutenant Colonel Tom Matthews could orchestrate whatever size force was needed, from the heavy option on down, to land and conduct the raid while the rest of the force remained in the air, ready to immediately assist, if needed.

In addition to the primary parts of the raid being conducted by the Delta assault force and two platoons of Rangers for the blocking positions, the task force had a number of other capabilities and parts of our team. Going in along with the assaulting force would be separate command elements for the Rangers and Delta. The Delta operators on the ground were commanded by the assault troop commander who was a major and, similarly, Captain Mike Steele would command the Ranger element from Bravo Company. Together, they would both be under Lieutenant Colonel Harrell, who was in command of the entire assault force, orbiting above in a Blackhawk helicopter.

Upon hearing this part of the plan, I recalled the books I had read about Vietnam and the many stories I had heard about the myriad problems that could occur when the commander was above the battle, flying in the C2 (command and control) bird, instead of on the ground. Hal Moore's briefing earlier that summer flashed through my mind, with his admonitions and emphasis on the importance of leadership being on the ground, before I quickly refocused on the brief.

Both Delta and the Rangers would also have fire support personnel. My fire support team would primarily support the Rangers and, as usual, I would be positioned with Captain Steele. I would have a Ranger FO at each of the four blocking positions around the target, and my team would also provide Ranger FOs for a planned convoy of vehicles, which was being organized to support the assault forces. Lastly, Sergeant Butch Galliete, brought along with me from Alpha Company, would be part of the Combat Search and Rescue (CSAR) team serving as their FO.

The Delta assault force, as was their practice, was supported by U.S. Air Force Combat Control Teams (CCTs) and one of their members, Tech Sergeant Jeff Bray, would be with their command element on the ground. USAF combat controllers were specialists in coordinating airstrikes, primarily from "fast mover" jets. As a backup, another one of the CCT members was assigned to stay with Captain Steele and me in the Ranger command element, working as part of my fire support team.

To provide additional support to the forces on the ground, two of the Blackhawk helicopters flying with the task force were designated to carry teams of Delta snipers. These aircraft, with their Delta snipers plus their standard door guns, would be directed onto threats by my FOs over the radio using basic fire support procedures. We would communicate with the pilots of the Blackhawks, giving them a cardinal direction or a compass azimuth, followed by a distance from our location. The pilots would fly over our position and engage the threat, based upon that information as well as requests that we would send them. As a backup to this plan, if one of the two Blackhawks carrying the Delta snipers had to come off station and leave or drop out for some reason, my aircraft Super 64 with its door gunners would come in and replace it. That would ensure we would always have two aircraft orbiting overhead, providing cover. From my perspective, the real ace in the hole for the task force was the presence of four AH-6 "Little Bird" attack helicopters in the aviation package. Small and nimble but heavily armed, these two-seat aircraft mounted Gatling guns and pods of 2.75-inch rockets.

Employing the AH-6 gunships in support of our missions was our normal practice, just as we had done during training at Fort Bliss. Each of the Ranger FOs in my team had worked extensively with the 160th and the gunships. However, directing Blackhawks with snipers on board was a relatively new approach for my Rangers and me. Even so, we would employ this new technique, as the task force had to follow the overall guidance from Washington, with a focus on maximum restraint. On most of the missions in Mogadishu, our AH-6 gunships would be limited to just being armed with their Gatling guns. They were not allowed to carry rockets on these missions unless specifically requested with justification and approval by the commanders. Another change for us was that, in order to conform to the normal practice of the U.S. Air Force CCT members supporting Delta, the Ranger forward observers would not be carrying our trusted FM radios but switching to UHF sets, which were a different type of radio with different capabilities. My Ranger FOs and I were leery and initially grumbled about this as it was a very fundamental equipment change.

Frequency modulating (FM) radios are primarily used by ground forces and, despite having a shorter range, they are very reliable in all kinds of terrain and conditions. Ultra-high frequency (UHF) radios rely on what is referred to as "line of sight." They have excellent range as long as the stations have a clear path between each other to communicate. Primarily used by aircraft, in the aviation world UHF would normally be the standard option. However, over years of training and working together with the Rangers and other ground forces, the 160th pilots and crews had incorporated the FM radios preferred by the ground forces into the array of systems on their aircraft. For the Rangers and the 160th, as with the rest of the Army, FM radios were the standard choice for air-to-ground communications. However, our concern about the radio system change was overruled and we were issued UHF radios, adding them to our gear. But along with these large, heavy radios, each FO also brought along a small, handheld FM radio as backup.

With our primary fire support being provided by the Delta snipers in Blackhawks flying overhead and the AH-6s from the 160th serving in reserve, we still had a number of other questions and concerns. Foremost among them was whether U.S. Air Force AC-130 gunships, which had for decades been included in any support package and special operations task force, would be approved to deploy and support this mission. The AH-6s we already had in the task force were ideal for bringing gunfire and rockets within meters of the troops on the ground. However, the amount of firepower provided by the AC-130, a four-engine, fixed-wing, armed transport plane with its 105mm main gun and array of other cannon and high-tech systems, was unparalleled in support of troops on the ground. We were told the AC-130 request had been made but the status of these aircraft was currently unknown. I was also concerned about the command structure and coordination between units with the Rangers on the perimeter and Delta on the target. Specifically, I was concerned with the coordination and approval of calling for fire support between the two elements of CCT and Ranger FOs.

In addition to the two platoons of Rangers and Delta operators going in with the assault force aboard the helicopters, another platoon of Rangers was organized into a mobile convoy of vehicles. Mounted in large military trucks and smaller HMMVs, this convoy would be available to move to the target area to provide reinforcements, and more firepower from .50-caliber machine guns and MK19 40mm automatic grenade launchers mounted on the vehicles. Bringing the convoy to the target area would also provide an option for the entire force to ride out of the area on the vehicles rather than having the helicopters return from their safe orbit and land in the target area. Two Ranger FOs rode on the Ranger convoy, to include my fire support team sergeant, Bill Powell, a Ranger veteran of Grenada.

Along with the Ranger convoy, another asset the task force had was a CSAR team as a contingency in case any of our aircraft crashed or were shot down. This team would fly along with the task force each time it launched aboard its own dedicated Blackhawk (Super 68) and was led by an experienced Ranger from B Company, Sergeant First Class Al Lamb. The CSAR was made up of a squad of Rangers as well as U.S. Air Force Pararescuemen (PJs). PJs are among the most skilled men in the U.S. military and are highly trained to deal with crash sites and medical emergencies. Sergeant Butch Galliete, who had come along with me from Alpha Company, was added to the CSAR team to provide fire support. Butch had been with me since he had first arrived in Alpha company as a young private, straight out of high school and initial Army training a few years earlier. In just over three years, we had been through a vast amount of training and experiences together. We had trained and deployed all over the world and met many challenges working together in Alpha Company. The shared experiences of the hard Ranger lifestyle and absolute dedication to the mission had forged a brotherhood that was similar to that of combat veterans. Beyond the iron discipline and uncompromising professionalism of the 75th Ranger Regiment, our comradeship and trust were absolute. I knew he would have my back, no matter what came, and it felt good to have him there as both of us were outsiders in B Company. As the limited number of positions in the task force were being assigned, I was glad to see Butch integrated into the CSAR team.

Lastly, in the organization of the task force, command of the operation in the immediate target area would be provided by the C Squadron commander, Lieutenant Colonel Gary Harrell, orbiting over the target in a C2 Blackhawk. Along with Harrell in the C2 bird would be the unit commander of all the task force helicopters from the 160th, Lieutenant Colonel Tom Matthews, who would handle and direct the aviation and complex air coordination aspects of the mission.

To simplify coordination among the various aviation elements, each type of aircraft received a standardized radio call sign based on its group and role. The attack helicopters, for example, were designated as a series of "Barber" aircraft, with each individual aircraft having a specific number. The radio call sign for the first AH-6 was "Barber 51," the second was "Barber 52," and so on, for each of the four Little Birds. Similarly, the MH-6s assigned to carry Delta operators were a series of "Star" call signs. Finally, the task force Blackhawks were given a series of "Super" call signs, beginning with "Super 61" and "Super 62," which were bringing in part of the Delta assault element. The command and control bird was "Super 63," and, continuing on through the four Blackhawks carrying the Rangers, we had "Super 64" through "67," with the CSAR bird being "Super 68."

As Lieutenant Colonel Harrell wrapped up his brief and with the basic outlines of a plan before us, we were anxious to get word back to the Rangers waiting in their tents at the camp. While there were still a number of lingering questions and issues to be worked out, we determined with the Delta leaders that the next step would be to link both units up and get out onto the training range, fall in on the mock-up buildings there, and begin to rehearse.

While we had finally been let in on the plan, we continued to try to catch up with C Squadron and build on the tenuous working relationships. Before leaving the Delta compound, Captain Steele and I walked around the facility, looking for some of the key leaders and trying to flesh out the information we had been given. We soon met the commander of SFOD-D, Colonel Jerry Boykin.

Boykin was a Vietnam veteran and highly experienced Delta officer. In addition to Vietnam, his combat resume included Operation *Eagle Claw*, the 1980 mission to rescue the American hostages in Iran, as well as the invasions of Grenada and Panama. During the invasion of Grenada in 1983, Boykin had been wounded in the shoulder by a .50-caliber round, while flying aboard a Blackhawk and leading an assault on the Richmond Hill Prison atop a steep mountain. He exuded experience and professional competence and we could not have had a better leader. Boykin's operations officer, referred to as the S3, was Major Ron Russell. Ron was another quiet professional who was very familiar to the Rangers. He had recently departed from us in 3rd Battalion, where he had been the S3 and then the executive officer (second in command) of the battalion for two years. In time, the

Delta leadership gave us more scraps of information as to what was going on and the immediate road ahead. Among other details, they informed us the official name of the mission would be Operation *Gothic Serpent*. About an hour later, we got in our vehicles and returned to the rest of the Rangers back in the tents at our camp nearby. After arriving there, we put out what information we had, then immediately began preparing for what would turn out to be a long series of intensive rehearsals at the ranges on Fort Bragg.

A key aspect of conducting any special operation is to "train like you fight" by rehearsing a plan as closely as possible to the actual conditions, to include using live ammunition. As we met C Squadron on the range, we began a "crawl-walk-run" approach. The Delta operators had been working on this plan for some time, but B Company was still working out the details. Similarly, the 160th SOAR aircraft had arrived and were ready, so we teamed up with our various aircraft and prepared to begin the initial walk-through rehearsals of the mission.

Each Ranger chalk was assigned to a Blackhawk helicopter and its crew. For the mission, we would fly in the same aircraft with the same crew, every time. In fact, we would standardize everything we possibly could, to include sitting in the same spot and exiting the aircraft in a choreographed sequence. The aircraft assigned to my group (R1), which included both the southeast blocking position and the company headquarters element led by

My parents, Jim and Sally, and I at The Citadel, Charleston South Carolina on Ring Night, 1988. (Author's collection)

The author serving as the fire support officer for Alpha Company, 3rd Battalion, 75th Ranger Regiment. pictured in front of a Ranger RSOV, or gun jeep, in 1991. (Author's collection)

Rangers from Alpha Company doing SPIE (special purpose insertion/extraction) rig from a Black Hawk helicopter during training at Elgin Air Force Base, Florida, in 1992. (Author's collection)

Alpha Company fire support team (FIST), with the author at the right and Butch Galliete second from left. (Author's collection)

Heavily armed Rangers sit on the edge of the doorway of Super 64 over Mogadishu.
(Author's collection)

A picture taken by the author from Super 64 while flying over Mogadishu in September
1993. Note the task force helicopters over the city in the distance. (Author's collection)

Rangers riding inside Black Hawk Super 64 during a mission over Mogadishu. Captain
Mike Steele is pictured in the center. (Author's collection)

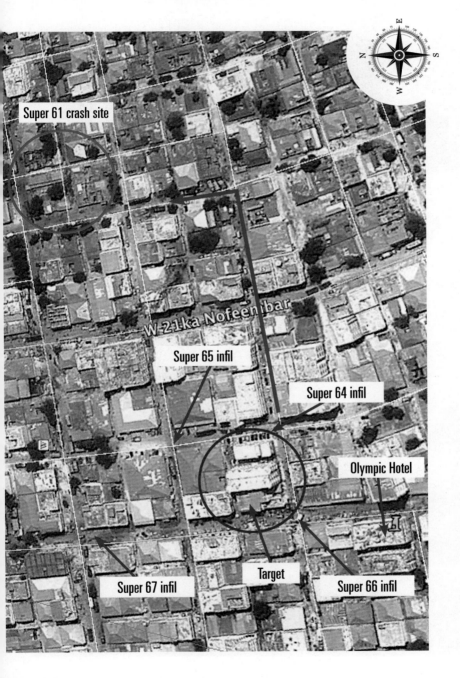

Red line shows the route taken by the assault force, including the author, from the target building to the Super 61 crash site.

Bravo Company, 3rd Battalion, 75th Ranger Regiment, in the desert
outside of Mogadishu in September 1993. (Author's collection)

The only picture taken from the ground during the battle. Shown is the target building
and Rangers of Chalks One and Four in the street in security perimeter.
(Author's collection)

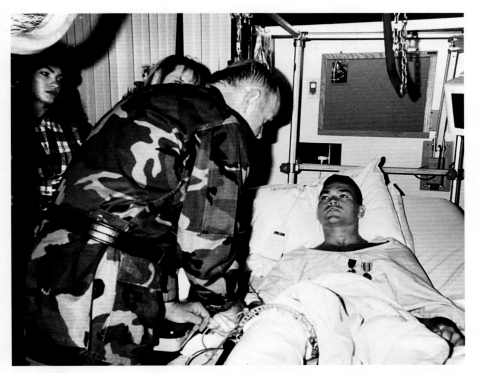

The Chief of Staff of the U.S. Army, General Gordon Sullivan, pins the Purple Heart on the author at Walter Reed Army Medical Center in October 1993, as his wife Beth and sister Amy look on. (Author's collection)

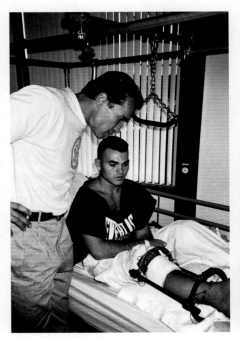

Left The author and Arnold Schwarzenegger at Walter Reed Army Medical Center, October 1993. (Author's collection)

Below The author and President Bill Clinton at Walter Reed Army Medical Center, October 1993. (The White House)

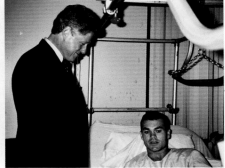

Members of Task Force Ranger stand in formation in front of the tactical operations center at Mogadishu Airport at a memorial service for their fallen comrades following the battle on October 3. (Courtesy 75th Ranger Regiment)

Above Mike Durant being carried to a medical evacuation aircraft by members of Task Force Ranger after his release in Mogadishu. (Courtesy US Special Operations Command)

Right The author's combat boot on display at the National Infantry Museum, Fort Benning, Georgia. This was worn when he was wounded on October 3, and the bloodstain shows the depth of pool of blood. (Author's collection)

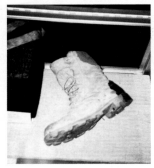

Captain Steele, was Super 64. Our pilots on Super 64 were my old comrade, Mike Durant, and a pilot I had not met before, Ray Franke, who, in addition to being a 160th veteran, had also served in Vietnam. The two crew chiefs were Sergeants Tom Fields and Bill Cleveland. Our aircrew were all great guys, professionals who were always calm and patient with us. We would spend a great deal of time together over the coming weeks and we quickly integrated into a cohesive team.

In accordance with the plan, the Delta operators would fly into the target divided between two types of aircraft. The assaulters, who would make initial contact on the ground, flew aboard MH-6 Little Bird aircraft. These were similar to AH-6 gunships but, instead of weapons, had bench seats mounted outside the airframe over the skids on which the Delta operators would ride, two on each bench. Besides the MH-6s, the remainder of Delta's assault element would fly on board two Blackhawk helicopters, while the four Ranger chalks would similarly fly aboard four Blackhawks of their own. For an assault, the small and nimble MH-6s could land in narrow city streets but the larger Blackhawks rarely could. In order to get the whole assault force on the ground, we would use the "fast-rope" technique. This meant attaching long ropes, as thick as a man's arm, to each side of the helicopter to be kept coiled inside during flight. Once the aircraft was over the target, the ropes would be kicked out to unwind down to the ground. While the pilots held the aircraft in a hover, the members of the assault force would pile out of the aircraft in sequence, grasping the rope tightly, and slide to the ground like firemen down a pole.

This was an extremely effective technique but it presented some challenges. The first was that the pilots had to keep the aircraft completely stable during the time it took everyone to exit, as the rope would sway with the movements of the aircraft. Missing the rope or merely not locking in a secure grip could mean a long fall to the ground below. An additional challenge was that, once on the rope, we had to remain stable, keeping a tight grip and sliding down without falling under not only our own bodyweight, but also all of our gear. We wore thick leather gloves for the descent but, often, still blistered our hands on the thick nylon ropes.

The weight became a significant issue. In addition to our standard helmets, each Ranger also wore heavy Kevlar and ceramic plate protective vests. Our Ranger uniform was the Army's tan and brown desert camouflage with its baggy trousers and blouse tops that hung down below our waists. We also wore the thick-soled, standard desert tan Army boots into which we tucked our baggy camouflage pants. We each had name tags and "U.S. Army" sewn over our breast pockets, which was standard for all uniforms. An additional point of pride was the reversed American flag, with the stars and blue field in the right (as opposed to left) upper corner, sewn onto the right shoulder of our uniforms. The American flag was worn this way by all

U.S. soldiers whenever they were deployed to a combat zone, dating back to at least World War II. By tradition, it was worn reversed so that it portrayed a flag always going forward. For missions, over our faded uniforms we wore our personal equipment, carrying magazines of ammunition and belts for the machine guns in pouches attached to our web belts. In other pouches, we carried fragmentation and smoke grenades, compasses, first aid kits, and strobe lights. Clipped to our pockets or hung on our belts were knives, red lens flashlights, and other tools. Strapped to our helmets were thick goggles needed during the shower of dust and debris kicked up by the intense rotor wash of the helicopters. Many Rangers carried other gear assigned by the platoon, such as anti-tank rockets and various other heavy equipment. For forward observers and radio operators, there was significantly more weight to carry, including the bulky UHF radios and batteries, all of which were added to the rucksacks on their backs. Still uneasy with the UHF sets, my FO team also carried the smaller handheld backup FM radios, in the cargo pockets on the side of the pants legs. Laden with our gear and with the outlines of the plan, we began to rehearse the details alongside the Delta operators.

We began with the basics, flying the entire assault force into a mock target in a relatively open grassy area. Sometimes, these first rehearsals would include "tape drills," with buildings being simulated and marked out on the grass represented by white engineer tape. The lead aircraft of the first wave with the Delta assault element would fly in and touchdown, or put their passengers out by fast-rope, then quickly peel off. They were soon followed by the second wave of four Blackhawks carrying the Rangers who would, similarly, fast-rope into the four corners around the target building. The four Ranger chalks were designated in sequence as R1 through R4. Each of these four individual groups of Rangers would be inserted into the same templated location every time. The template itself was applied based upon the cardinal direction and orientation of the target and surrounding area. In other words, with north as a common reference, on every mission R1 would fast-rope into the southeast corner, R2 would go into the northeast, R3 into the northwest, and R4 into the southwest. As we rehearsed this part of the assault over and over, it began to become intuitive. Once you made it to the ground, following the chaos and violence of the fast-rope descent from the hovering Blackhawks, all you had to do was use your compass, figure out which direction was north, and the pieces would all fall into place. Then, facing outward in a protective perimeter, the Rangers would keep the target building and Delta operators behind them. Each Ranger blocking position would have two adjacent Ranger blocking positions to their left and right, tying in the entire force of Rangers surrounding the target together in a square. This perimeter served to shield the Delta operators from interference as they breached and cleared the buildings inside the perimeter.

Once established, the perimeter would also act as a net to catch any Somali trying to flee the target buildings during the mission.

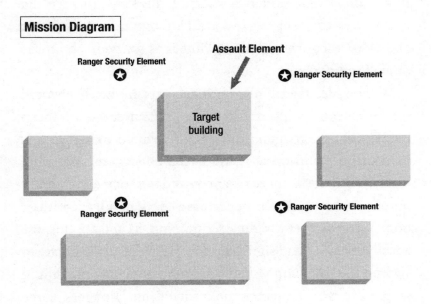

Over the next few days, we rehearsed this mission profile numerous times until it became automatic. The commanders quickly increased the complexity of the rehearsals, running scenarios during the night, using our weapons with live ammunition, and throwing in various contingencies and surprises. With the advantages of our night vision equipment, the darkness of night missions was our preferred venue. In addition to target buildings, we worked on assaulting vehicles in both large convoys or down to a single car. The commanders tried to carefully think through every reasonable contingency and we practiced dealing with casualties and holding back large mobs, as well as coordinated attacks on our perimeter. At this point in our understanding of the situation, we did not expect to meet a great deal of organized resistance and were as concerned about rioters as we were about the Somali militiamen.

We conducted multiple rehearsals each night, then would return to our open-air tents to catch a few hours' sleep before beginning again in daylight. We were used to this kind of pace and these rustic living conditions. We were just happy to have cots to sleep on and hot food and it didn't bother us that the Delta operators were going back to their homes nearby every night after training. To a man, this was exactly what we had signed up for. We were all desperate to stay on the team and would offer no complaints that might jeopardize that. However, unknown to the Rangers, some of the Delta staff officers began to grumble for us about our living conditions. This was of particular concern to Major John "Doc" Marsh, the SFOD-D surgeon and son of the Secretary of the Army. His complaints to the command would eventually bear fruit for us in the form of better conditions but, for the time being, we were happy in our tents and focused on the mission.

As we continued the intensive schedule of rehearsing through the night hours, the weight we carried on the mission continued to be an issue. We all had close calls coming down the fast-ropes and, soon, the assault force began to lose Rangers to injuries from the hard landings with broken ankles and legs. We had reached the limits of our physical ability to be able to both fast-rope and to carry the amount of gear we needed on the mission. So, naturally, we began to look for ways to lighten the load by thinking through priorities and the mission parameters. In other words, what would you need to fight and stay alive and what might you be able to live without for a short time? Some hard choices had to be made as we continued the rehearsals. This process of mission assessment and tough decision-making on equipment continued throughout the deployment and for nearly every mission.

As the days of incessant training went on at Fort Bragg, we periodically heard reports on the discussions and direction coming from Washington, D.C. about the deployment of the task force. The first disappointing update we received while still training at Fort Bragg was the news that the U.S. Air Force AC-130 gunship would not be included in the task force. Some of the gunships had been previously deployed to the region and operated over Mogadishu flying from a base in Kenya. However, by August, their tour was complete and Secretary of Defense Les Aspin made the decision to bring the aircraft home. Coupled with our expectations of little Somali resistance, the tone being set from Washington was for the maximum amount of restraint to be exercised on the missions. This was not the last time I would experience this attitude from the

Clinton Administration. Their desire was for the mission to be conducted with as little military action as possible, minimizing the impact on civilian bystanders, whose injury or death was often referred to as "collateral damage." It seemed keeping the AC-130 on station to support the task force would be too aggressive – too much unnecessary firepower from Washington's perspective. Similarly, the Pentagon had rejected our request for armored vehicles as an additional asset to move the assault force through the streets of Mogadishu. In spite of these disappointments, we had worked out many of the gaps and rough spots in the plan after the extensive rehearsals with C Squadron and our helicopter crews. After multiple rehearsals during the day and night with various scenarios thrown in, we had ensured that the overall plan for the assault force was well coordinated and flexible. Abruptly, in the midst of this training, the key leaders of the task force were summoned to the Delta compound.

As the Rangers and operators assembled in Delta's plush dining facility (DFAC), we were met by Colonel Boykin. He had a new and disturbing update from Washington. He bluntly informed us that the mission was being cancelled. B Company and the rest of the Rangers were to depart immediately and rejoin the rest of 3rd Battalion back at Fort Bliss. That was it. Colonel Boykin went on to praise our hard work and our dedication, urging us to stay focused as we didn't know what the future would hold. That afternoon, we broke camp in our small tent city and quickly loaded USAF transports. We soon took off, flying west back to Fort Bliss.

Arriving back in Texas that evening, Butch Galliete and I walked into the Alpha Company area and began to settle in, providing short answers to all inquiries, just as we had been directed. But before we could unpack our rucks, in what was now becoming a pattern in this drama, a messenger arrived from battalion headquarters. A new order had come from Washington. We were to immediately rejoin B Company. The mission was a GO! But there were also more changes. The additional Rangers from 1st Platoon, Alpha Company, had been cut by officials in Washington. Saying quick goodbyes to a disappointed 1st Platoon and my FO, Sergeant Lessner, we headed back to join B Company. Within hours, we were again reloading the waiting USAF transport aircraft and were soon flying back across the country to Fort Bragg.

Touching down at Fort Bragg, we found that all of the Rangers were now being billeted inside the Delta compound. The concerns of the good Doctor Marsh on our behalf were met and the Rangers were given quarters in the long squadron equipment bays where cots had been set up and the air conditioning hummed in the background.

Almost immediately, we began the rituals of deploying soldiers — final medical checks and the semi-invasive shot regimen in our rear lower extremities. We did last administrative checks to ensure our affairs were in order. However, this did not take long as we had gotten our paperwork and affairs in order earlier in the summer when we assumed RRF1. The evening before our departure, all of the task force came through the compound's first-class dining facility for a steak dinner and huge spread. After that, there was one final somber pre-deployment ritual to complete. Every Ranger was given paper, pen, and an envelope and told to write some parting thoughts to loved ones.

I had not completely digested the shock and excitement of the last few days, with all of the dramatic ups and downs. Just over two months ago, I had been single. Now, I was married with a baby on the way and, instead of heading to a classroom at Fort Benning, I was with B Company and Task Force Ranger about to embark on the odyssey of my life. With these thoughts in the back of my mind, I tried to compose my letter to Beth, writing down my love for her, but also how thrilled and stunned I was to be deploying. To this point, none of us had been able to call our families and we remained in a communications "blackout," a security parameter which always surrounded top secret JSOC missions. However, we knew many of them had seen the news reports of the pending U.S. special operations response to events in Somalia and so they knew something was in the works. We sealed our letters and, leaving part of our legacy in those envelopes, handed them off to the clerks and chaplains.

The next day, the entire task force was broken down into groups of deployment chalks, then moved to the airfield aboard buses driven by support personnel from Delta. Each chalk piled out of the buses and climbed the lowered ramps leading onto huge C-5 transport aircraft. The chalks would travel separately, spaced over the next 72 hours, to arrive in Mogadishu after brief refueling stops in Germany. Our helicopters and pallets of equipment and ammunition were packed in the cavernous lower spaces of the C-5s. After walking up the huge rear ramp of the C-5s, we climbed the steep ladders to the aircraft's upper deck to find comfortable, cloth padded seats. I took a seat next to one of the Delta operators, Steve Cashen. Steve was an intellectual warrior, extremely fit, skilled, and smart. We had common interests in a number of areas, to include German history, so we spent hours talking on the long flight. Like many other special operators, Steve and I would continue to meet on battlefields for decades to come.

Almost immediately after the C-5 took off, we got word from the Air Force crew that the big transport had lost one of its engines with a mechanical failure. Though we could continue on this leg of the flight without it, upon landing at Ramstein, Germany, our flight was delayed so the problem could be fixed. We were forced to sit for hours on an isolated ramp while mechanics changed out the bad engine. With a new engine but having lost half a day, we finally departed Germany and continued on our way. Our delay en route caused us to be among the last of the task force aircraft to arrive in Mogadishu. On the approach to the airport, we could not see much of the city through the small portholes of the aircraft, just streaks of dusty gray and brown of the desert, contrasting sharply with flashes of deep blue from the Indian Ocean. Finally, near the end of August, the huge transport touched down on the worn runway and into the reality of Mogadishu.

5

On the Hunt

Vekka yðr at víni   I wake you not to wine
né at vífs rúnum,   nor to women's talk,
heldr vekk yðr at hörðum   but rather to the hard
Hildar leiki.   game of Hild.*

Bjarkamál Skaldic Poem 1000 AD

After our C-5 aircraft touched down in Mogadishu and
came to a halt, we got off the plane and walked onto
the concrete of the airfield tarmac. Looking around at
the dusty brown landscape and surrounding airfield,
we saw rubbled buildings and the hulks of wrecked and
abandoned aircraft strewn among piles of garbage. Off
to the north, we saw a large tent city and the shacks that
comprised the United Nations compound, which housed
U.S. military and forces from other countries including
Italy, Egypt, and Australia. To our immediate rear, just
a few hundred yards away, were the blue waters of the
Indian Ocean. To our front, at the south end of the airfield,

* Hild was a Norse Valkyrie of battle.

was a rundown, two-story building. Not far behind this building, the walls of the airfield perimeter and the dense urban sprawl of the city neighborhoods looked down on us. Bristling with radio antennae and camouflage netting, we guessed the building to our front was the task force (TF) headquarters and tactical operations center (TOC). Alongside the TOC was a large dilapidated hangar and a cluster of new white trailers. Carrying our gear, we were led through the growing maze of razor wire and sandbags, past the white trailers, and through piles of rubble into the dark hangar. The cave-like space would be home for the duration of our tour in Somalia. We dropped our gear, lined up cots, and began what would become the never-ending process of cleaning and repairing the interior of the hangar. Almost the entire 450-man task force would be housed there, sleeping on long rows of cots inside the hangar. C Squadron would take the back left, the Rangers of B Company the right, and the ground crews of the 160th were arrayed along the front. Besides the most senior commanders who stayed in the TOC building, the exception to these arrangements were the helicopter pilots, who were housed next door in the new white, air-conditioned trailers. As their flying skills and mental acuity meant life or death for us riding in the back of the aircraft, we had no complaints about this arrangement, wanting them fresh and well rested for every mission.

Over the next few days, we began to size up our living conditions at the airfield while also immediately focusing on the mission at hand. The August heat along the equator in Africa surpassed even that of the Texas desert, broken only by the occasional sea breeze. We could see the ocean across the airfield, not far from where we sweltered in our small compound. In the heat, the Delta operators and many of the 160th aircrew stripped down to shorts and t-shirts. But the uniform discipline of the Rangers remained initially in place. The Rangers gritted their teeth and continued to set up the area and man the perimeter barricades in our desert camouflage uniforms.

By August 26, the entire TF had arrived in Mogadishu and the key leaders had begun to regularly assemble and receive updates in the TOC building. Gradually, the bigger picture of the task force became apparent to us. In the TOC, we soon met Major General Bill Garrison who was the commander of Joint Special Operations Command and would now command the overall effort of Task Force Ranger. The same leaders who had assembled with us at Fort Bragg – Lieutenant Colonel McKnight (3rd Ranger Battalion commander), Lieutenant Colonel Harrell (C Squadron commander), and Colonel Boykin (commanding SFOD-D) – each had his role to play and would assist Major General Garrison, but the overall responsibility and command was his.

Bill Garrison was a tall Texan who seemed grizzled and somewhat aged to us young Rangers. He had a wealth of experience as a veteran of Vietnam, where he had been part of the Phoenix Program. After the war he had helped found Delta under its legendary first commander, Colonel Charlie Beckwith. Major General Garrison quietly paced around the TOC or stood outside watching the constant activity of the soldiers of the TF, but did not insert himself into the direction of individuals or units. Instead, he was a constant and vigilant presence, leaning on a wall in the back of briefings. He knew he had plenty of competent leaders and kept his focus on the "macro" process of hunting for Aideed and responding to phone calls from the brass at the Pentagon, who sought constant updates.

Along with the additional command element from JSOC, we began to grasp the scope of the effort to hunt Aideed. Our primary intelligence collection platform was a U.S. Navy P-3 Orion anti-submarine warfare plane. The sensors on this slow-flying submarine hunter were repurposed for locating General Aideed within the city. In accordance with the standard Cold War methods used against our Soviet adversaries, the P-3 would listen closely for any radio communications Aideed might make. In addition to this signals intelligence (SIGINT), there was a growing network of spies and other operatives being recruited and sent out to the Habr Gidr areas. Aideed's personal ambitions and resistance to the UN had not only cost the Habr Gidr scores of casualties but also cut off access to relief efforts. This, combined with his ruthless leadership of the Habr Gidr clan in the conflict and heavy hand with dissenters, had made Aideed a number of enemies. These discontented members of the Habr Gidr clan were the ideal recruits to help us get to Aideed. Their cooperation was secured with promises of pay and a share of the $25,000 reward now being offered.

The United Nations forces, led by the U.S. military, had been conducting intensive intelligence efforts to pick up the trail of Aideed throughout the spring and summer. With the arrival of Task Force Ranger in Mogadishu, these efforts were now given a priority at the national level, direct from the President of the United States. This prioritization brought with it a variety of intelligence assets, to include a number of highly specialized and equipped reconnaissance helicopters flown by Task Force Ranger pilots. These aircraft could quickly respond from our base at the airfield and run down leads provided by the P-3 or reports from locally recruited spies. With incredibly high-tech cameras and targeting equipment, these aircraft could track and provide positive identification of Aideed or any other target, once they had come into the overall intelligence net.

Much of this effort evolved over the weeks the task force spent searching for Aideed in Mogadishu and eventually developed into an effective intelligence system. However, in the very first days as Task Force Ranger was getting established on the ground in Mogadishu and getting acclimated, we were essentially limited to what intelligence the UN forces could give us. Our own intelligence personnel began to provide frequent briefings and updates on the deteriorating situation in the city. Unfortunately, they had little to share on the whereabouts of our main target, General Aideed. He had last been seen weeks before at a large chaotic rally, exhorting his clansmen to resist the United States before disappearing back into the shadows of the vast Habr Gidr ghetto with his militiamen. The initial awkward attempts by the UN forces to capture Aideed earlier that year had merely served to alert the SNA and drive Aideed underground. The Western media, for their part, were aware of the deteriorating situation between Aideed and the UN and aggressively trolled for information on the task force. With more sensitive information invariably being exposed as the special operators and Rangers arrived in Mogadishu, the military attempted to establish an overall cover, referring to us as Task Force Ranger. This designation was based upon the Rangers' obvious participation and was intended as a screen for the rest of the special operations forces involved in the mission. These overt public affairs measures also included putting Lieutenant Colonel McKnight out in front of the microphones upon his arrival in Mogadishu, to make generic platitudes as to our purpose here. Aideed paid close attention to all of this and was not fooled.

General Mohamed Farah Aideed of the Habr Gidr clan had previously served in the Somali Army. There, he received formal military training, first from the Italians during their colonial administration, and later more extensively from the Soviets during their time in Somalia.

With increasing awareness and perception of the U.S. efforts to capture him, Aideed was extremely savvy to standard intelligence approaches and capabilities Task Force Ranger would employ to track and locate him, such as our reliance on radio interception or SIGINT. In response to our efforts, Aideed took a number of extremely effective countermeasures. He completely abstained from radio or telephone communications, instead passing written or verbal messages through his most trusted subordinates.

Aideed knew that the task force was on his trail and that remaining static, staying in one place, or setting a consistent pattern was what would give us the best opportunity for locating him. Just the smallest indicator or thread of information could lead us to his location and an opportunity to capture him.

Aideed was fully aware of his vulnerability and he made maximum use of his greatest advantage and blended in to the homogenous clan network of the Habr Gidr in Mogadishu. He never stayed in the same house for more than a few nights and relied upon trusted relatives. Similarly, he never set an easily identifiable pattern in his activities, some days moving around in large, well-guarded convoys, and others in just a single vehicle. Aideed used cover and disguise to hide, including dressing as a woman. The militiamen who served as his security force also used sound tactics and methods, such as sending an advance party to Aideed's destinations to scout them out and secure them before he arrived. They also attempted to block roads and limit UN access, screening the movements of Aideed through the city. In addition to these efforts, Aideed proactively sent his supporters to clandestinely penetrate not only UN organizations but inside the Task Force Ranger compound, posing as contract and sanitation workers and gleaning any information they could to report back to Aideed. Many of Aideed's security and intelligence efforts had already been underway. Now, with the well-publicized arrival of Task Force Ranger, they were refocused and intensified.

Meanwhile, back in the TOC in the first days after our arrival, we studied old Soviet maps hung on the walls and satellite imagery of the city. We also read reports from the other U.S. forces in Mogadishu, mainly from the 10th Mountain Division, and we grilled the occasional officers who visited from outside the TF. After a visit to the headquarters of the 10th Mountain Division forces at the nearby university compound, we exchanged liaison officers with them to try to better coordinate efforts between our units. Representing Task Force Ranger and acting as liaison for us with the other U.S. forces was my first Ranger commander from Alpha Company, Craig Nixon, newly promoted to major.

After leaving the company two years earlier, Craig had gone off to a tour in Korea at the famous Demilitarized Zone. Now, in the summer of 1993, he was newly arrived back at 3rd Ranger Battalion, just in time to join us for the deployment to Somalia. He would be a cool-headed conduit to the other U.S. forces and help smooth the natural frictions and tensions of a special operations task force inserting into the middle of their operations in Mogadishu. In return, the 10th Mountain sent us Lieutenant John Breen, a fellow fire supporter who would give us unvarnished assessments of his views on the situation.

On one of my first nights in Mogadishu, John took me on one of the aerial patrols being conducted around the clock by Army Blackhawk helicopters assigned to the 10th Mountain. We flew over the sprawling darkness of the city that night for two and a half hours, seeing little movement or contact on the ground. When the Blackhawks initially took off and rose above the rooftops, it was shocking to see the absence of lighting or electric power among the crowded mass of almost a million people. The city landscape was a blackened sprawl of burning fires, casting shadows on the rubbled buildings and deserted streets with only the occasional generator-driven white lights of the rich or in the UN military camps. It was surreal at best and a testament to how far this city and nation had fallen into the chaotic abyss.

Almost immediately, Task Force Ranger began to look for aggressive outlets, with the Delta operators and Rangers prowling around the immediate vicinity of our compound on the airfield. As we waited tensely for intelligence to give us a target, we began to resume training and look for ways to push out of the confines of the airfield. Occasionally, Somali gunmen would take pot shots at the outer perimeter of the airfield, manned by Egyptian Army soldiers with the UN, or conduct light probes against the other UN forces situated on the northeastern end of the airfield. These included U.S. Army aviation units, an Italian Army contingent, and a hodgepodge of other western European and Australian support units. On our second night at the airfield, Aideed's militia, aware of our presence, welcomed us with an inaccurate smattering of mortar rounds that landed mostly along the adjacent beachfront. The next night, the mortars improved their aim and walked rounds across the airfield tarmac just outside our wire, slightly wounding one TF soldier. They gave us a departing gesture by "shacking" one round onto the concrete roof of the TOC. As a fire supporter, part of me was perversely thrilled to be "mortared" for the first time, but I tried to respond coolly and professionally. Jogging out in the direction from which we had heard the impact, I scanned the tarmac for the distinctive jagged hole made by a mortar round on impact. Soon finding one of the jagged crescent-shaped shell holes, I began conducting a "crater analysis" to determine the originating point of the rounds. Taking a bearing from the center of the crater back toward the direction it had been fired, I used my map and compass to determine its point of origin. The results were predictable, pointing north, into the nearest Habr Gidr neighborhood.

Not having a clear target and little other intelligence on the attack, the TF began to react in a knee-jerk manner. One platoon of Rangers was sent on patrol into the streets outside the airfield but with no result.

Then, around midnight, Major General Garrison quietly directed the assault force to be assembled. As the key leaders, including Captain Steele, the other Ranger chalk leaders and me, arrived in the TOC, we were given the word we would be launching against the top Habr Gidr/ SNA target from the list recently given to us by the 10th Mountain Division. The target was a building called the Lig Ligato House and was thought to be a center of SNA operations. This mission would begin with the quick planning process to set and orchestrate our assault using satellite imagery of the target building, in conjunction with our mission template and based upon the extensive rehearsals we had conducted at Fort Bragg. My friend, Jim Klingaman, working as a staff officer in the TOC, now secured a key role in the planning for these missions. As the intelligence on the target developed, Jim observed the imagery and video as it came in "real time" from our surveillance aircraft. He then immediately drew the target area in a sketch on a large dry erase board placed in front of the assembled leaders. Within the tight confines of the briefing space, the key leaders of each Delta assault element stepped up to the board and, using the sketch, described how they would enter or "breach" and assault the target building. Following that, the lead helicopter pilots quickly pointed out some issues, prompting adjustments to be made. The Rangers, as rehearsed, simply took the outside four corners and set the perimeter based upon these plans. Within minutes of these coordinations, copies of the sketch were printed and everyone moved back to the hangar.

Posted in front of the hangar waiting on the key leaders to return, First Sergeant Glenn Harris got the nod from Captain Steele, then, turning to the waiting Rangers, thundered, "Get it on!" Within seconds, the waiting Rangers and Delta operators strapped on protective vests and personal gear, set their helmets with night vision goggles, and loaded their weapons. In that confined space, the sound of steel rifle bolts slamming home to load weapons while over 200 of the world's finest soldiers strapped on armor and set their helmets, was exhilarating and sublime. It set off a current of excitement and tension that continued to build as each member of the assault force moved to join his small team and then formed chalks as we strode out to the lines of aircraft on the tarmac. As our chalk found Super 64, we could dimly make out the faint gold lettering of its name, "Venom," painted above the open doorway of the helicopter. The helicopter engines were already beginning their shrill, high-pitched whine as our aircrew conducted pre-flight checks and Rangers began to load up and find their designated spots on the floor of the Blackhawks. Those of us on the inside spaces of the aircraft quickly snapped our safety lines into rings on the floor before the remainder of the chalk packed in, sitting on the edges of the two doorways. We grabbed their equipment harnesses and held on to ensure they stayed firmly planted inside the birds. The excess lengths of the heavy green fast-ropes that hung suspended above the doorways were piled in tight coils among the outer row of Rangers. My spot was on the left side of the bird with my back against the firewall and pressed against the Rangers sitting on the outer edge. From there, I was able to partially see through the windshield and the backs of the heads of the two pilots, Mike Durant and Ray Frank. The crew chiefs sat directly behind the pilots, each facing outward and manning their Gatling guns that, if needed, could be used to provide an incredible amount of fire (between two and four thousand rounds per minute) to help suppress the enemy as we came in to land or to support actions on the ground. Kevlar blankets had been laid on the floor of the Blackhawks, giving us some protection from below. This allowed me to rationalize against the classic Vietnam era move of sitting on my helmet. From my position, I could also see out the open doorway to my left as the rotor blades of the task force picked up and began to spin. Captain Steele was seated forward along the centerline of the bird, not far behind the pilots, while the chalk leader, my friend Lieutenant Larry Perino, was jammed in next to him. Steele had his helmet off and wore a radio headset, communicating with the pilots and monitoring their radio traffic with the commanders. We sat sweating inside the Blackhawk in spite of the night air, which grew heavier with the smell of engine oil and exhaust. We now had 17 Rangers packed into Super 64 and each one waited tensely for the launch order, not sure if it would be given. After all the alerts and cancellations over the past weeks, we sat sweating another scratch of the mission. Suddenly, the engines began to strain while, simultaneously, Captain Steele made excited gestures that the launch order was given. Above the noise of the engines, I could hear the Rangers cheering as we lifted off into the night.

As the mass of aircraft rose lumbering into the night, they soon picked up the usual formation. The pilots had flown so often during the endless rehearsals they came together almost instinctively. The lead Blackhawks and MH-6s, carrying the Delta operators faintly silhouetted in the dark sky, paced off into the lead while the remainder of the Blackhawks trailed behind. As we made a quick turn around the city and headed east, Chief Cliff Wolcott, piloting the lead Blackhawk Super 61, almost immediately picked up the sparkle of laser markings reflecting off the target area through his night vision goggles. These laser markings were being provided by our recon aircraft onto the target building to help guide us in. Now the mass of Rangers in our aircraft began to shift and tense as our pilots slowed Super 64 into a hover, easing into our position for insertion. Chemlite sticks, fastened to the ends of the fast-ropes, were cracked and came alight so that, when dropped, the lead Ranger and crew chief could confirm the bird was all the way down and resting on solid ground. Amid the roar of the aircraft engines, unintelligible orders were shouted and the ropes went out while Rangers strained to grasp them and hang on before disappearing into the blackness and dust as we exited in a controlled surge. I took one half-step from my seated position, then, reaching for the rope, I locked it in as my arms caught my weight and I slid down. That first "combat rope" was not exceptionally high but a giant leap for all of us as we crossed the threshold of experience for which every professional soldier aches.

This would be the first real-world mission for many of us and, fortunately, it passed with few hitches. By the time we sorted out the Ranger blocking positions in the dark, the Delta operators were well into the clearance of the buildings. The Rangers established the perimeter and we caught glimpses in the dark of the Delta operators moving around the target building. They soon emerged with a handful of prisoners, blindfolded and with their hands tied with thin plastic flex cuffs. The Somalis timidly knelt against a wall, guarded by Delta operators as the clearing teams began to come out of the target building. After about 30 minutes on the ground, Delta had the building completely cleared, the Somali prisoners secured, and were prepared to move. The decision was then made to extract the entire force on helicopters, which would land in a small adjacent courtyard. There was a metal pole obstructing the space and, after a few abortive attempts, it was finally cleared with a demolition charge. Even after the pole was taken down, I looked at the tiny space with skepticism. As I stood observing and did the mental math on the space needed for a Blackhawk, one of the smaller MH-6s made a tricky approach to the space, first dropping below an overhang, then weaving into the relatively flat spot for a pick up. We remained incredulous even as Wolcott confirmed he would put his Blackhawk on the ground there next. As the bird eased, shark-like, into the courtyard, the rotors crackled and glowed with static electricity. The clearance on at least one wall seemed like inches and I turned my face away in apprehension. Almost immediately, I felt a rough hand on my shoulder as Captain Steele spun me around and pushed me toward the door of the aircraft. The Blackhawk was still settling into the dust as we moved forward to load in the back. The assault force had been on the ground for less than an hour. After a short flight back, we landed at the still-dark airfield. Streaming off the aircraft, the key leaders broke off and quickly moved toward the TOC to conduct our post-mission "hotwash" brief, while the rest of the operators and Rangers headed to the hangar. Our Somali prisoners had been lifted out before the assault force. Immediately flown to the airfield, they had been processed and moved to a small razor-wire enclosure adjacent to the hangar.

The mood in the TOC was calm and almost anticlimactic. The UN headquarters had responded to the raid with a surprising report that identified our prisoners as UN workers and the Lig Ligato House was their office. As we tried to process this news, a number of questions were immediately raised. Was this the right house? What about the reported SNA activity? We had hit the right building and it was in fact owned by Osman Atto, Aideed's number two man and chief financier. Atto rented the building to the UN during the day and, after hours, occasionally conducted SNA business at the location. This illicit nighttime activity was what had generated the intelligence reports. Unfortunately, on this particular evening, there had been no SNA meetings but some of the hapless UN workers had chosen the wrong night to stay late. They were in the right place at the wrong time. For us, it was a rude welcome to the complexities of Mogadishu. We also took it as a valuable lesson about the risks of working off other people's intelligence and target development. These lessons would later serve me well on numerous other operations from Bosnia to Iraq and Afghanistan.

As the post-mission hotwash inside the TOC began to break up, I walked over to Cliff Wolcott, the mission lead for 160th. Cliff was an Army chief warrant officer, a rank midway between regular commissioned officers and sergeants. He had vast experience and skill as a pilot. The aviation world, while still part of the military, was a very different culture than the Ranger Regiment. Their organizations had officers in command of their companies and platoons but these were more administrative duties. For missions, the flight leads were designated from the pilots who had the most experience and demonstrated skill, regardless of rank. Cliff was not only an amazing pilot but had a big personality, and with his shock of brown hair was given the nickname "Elvis." He was never afraid to voice his opinion, but he was also always fun to be around. I told Cliff I had been skeptical about him getting his Blackhawk into the tiny landing zone back at the target and how amazed I had been watching him bend the laws of physics to land successfully. Cliff smiled and said, "Just watch and learn, Lieutenant."

While the media gleefully described our first raid as a "bungled operation" and the UN expressed their displeasure, Major General Garrison took a patient step back and exercised mature discretion. The task force had reacted, in part, to Aideed's goading with the mortars and probes and had failed to immediately grasp the subtleties of tracking him in the city. We quickly realized that on this type of operation there would be no looming forts to assault or flags to capture. Only careful study of patterns and vulnerabilities, while waiting on opportunities for a quick strike, would lead us to success. This would be accomplished by continuing to weave our intelligence net, casting it throughout the city and building the picture of where to find Aideed, day after day, week after week.

We also began to realize we would get little assistance from the UN forces in Mogadishu. On the contrary, they seemed to be drawing back from the conflict more with each passing week. As Major General Garrison and Colonel Boykin led the staff through these assessments and developments, the Rangers and operators of the task force waited restlessly. In order to keep us focused on our singular purpose, the task force was reined in from any more patrols or actions outside of the airfield beyond what was required for resupply and logistics. In any case, the commanders in the TOC had another role for us to play.

In order to mitigate the obvious signs of a mission being launched when the task force helicopters rose in a thundering mass from the airfield, we began to conduct "signature flights." At least once a day, and often twice, the entire force would saddle up like we were heading out on a mission, loading our helicopters and flying around the city at various times of the day or night. Aboard our modern helicopters, flown by the best pilots in the world, we exulted in the raw power and speed of the flights, roaring above the Somali neighborhoods at rooftop level. Wagner's "Flight of the Valkyries" would be cliché, but absolutely applicable, to illustrate the experience of flying with that assault force. Catching glimpses of Somalis on the ground, often close enough to make eye contact, we left dust, debris, and sheets of metal roofing cascading in our wake.

In addition to the signature flights, the assault force kept busy training. While the Delta operators built obstacle courses and shooting ranges, B Company began an intensive training program, travelling almost daily to the nearby desert sand dunes and conducting shooting ranges and small scale live fires. My fire support team and I similarly continued to work on our skills in the desert, directing the company's 60mm mortars and calling in the AH-6 Little Birds. We set up ranges and built targets using former Somali Army vehicles that we scavenged, along with other debris that we found amid the wreckage and ruins of the airfield.

While the signature flights and training ranges occupied much of our days and nights, the task force continued to work hard, trying to develop intelligence on Aideed. While Aideed's countermeasures, such as staying off the radio, were often very effective, a few cracks began to appear in his armor. Informers and spies began to leak information of his meetings and "bed down" locations. This slow trickle of reports and tips was just enough to keep the assault force on frequent alert. This often included moving through the stages of assembling key leaders, developing plans, sometimes even loading aircraft. But rarely was the threshold or "trigger" met to confirm the viability of making an assault.

Then, on September 6, we received a promising lead from a spy who reported that Aideed would bed down in a complex of buildings called the old Russian Compound. While our reconnaissance aircraft could not positively identify Aideed at the location, the report was the best we had received to that point in our efforts. The commanders made the decision to load the helicopters and launch the assault force a few hours after dark. Graduating through the increasing stages of alert until the final word to "go" was almost instinctive now as we quickly loaded onto our birds. After a few minutes in the air flying over the city, the assault force began to descend into an area with wide boulevards. The old Russian Compound was adjacent to a large thoroughfare, which gave the assault force the luxury of touching down in our helicopters and foregoing the hazardous fast-ropes.

As usual, the birds with the Delta assault teams landed first, followed closely by the Ranger Blackhawks landing in a line along the wide street. Our chalk piled out of the right side of the Blackhawk, spreading out in the darkness and pushing through ditches and scrub brush up to the walls of the compound. Once on the ground at the target area, the assault force entered a confusing warren of barracks-type buildings amid pervading darkness. As the Delta operators cleared buildings, then reoriented themselves and cleared more, the Rangers put in their blocking positions as best we could in the dark. To my left, one team of two Rangers reported just being able to make out the adjacent blocking position down the alleyway. Even with our night vision goggles, we were able to see very little in the darkness amid the tight network of buildings and numerous piles of rubble. Under the direction of the chalk leader, Lieutenant Perino, the Rangers at our blocking position pushed out a short distance from where Captain Steele and I remained kneeling by the compound wall. Still trying to identify and tie in with the Rangers to our left and right, we oriented our weapons down the narrow alleys and covered the approaching paths around us. After about 30 minutes of tense waiting, the Somalis began to react and came looking for us. Stumbling along without night vision goggles, they probed the darkness around the target compound. First, a quick exchange of shots down an alley near our blocking position, then the boom of RPGs (rocket-propelled grenades) off in the distance. The RPGs were immediately followed by a roar of heavy automatic weapons fire. One of the blocking positions near us had responded to a Somali probe, while at almost the same time, the Rangers of 3rd Platoon in the vehicle convoy had made contact a few blocks away.

On this mission, Major General Garrison had launched the convoy of HMMVs and trucks manned by the Rangers and commanded by Lieutenant Colonel McKnight to support the assault force. Rather than immediately bringing them into the confused darkness around the Olympic Village, the commanders held the convoy a short distance away, out on the main road, waiting for the order to move forward and pick up the assault force. Along with the enemy, who had bumped into our blocking position, other Somalis searching for the assault force had stumbled into the convoy waiting along the road position. They had prematurely launched RPGs and engaged with at least one light machine gun. The Ranger platoon's response was violent and overwhelming, with .50-caliber machine guns and MK19 grenade launchers shredding the Somali position. The short, almost one-sided exchanges, had been the first real contact for the Rangers. One of the Rangers on the convoy, Specialist Joe Harosky, received a light wound to the leg from some of the RPG fragments, and Sergeant Mike Pringle, standing in the turret of the battalion commander's HMMV, had his helmet spun around by a machine-gun bullet. Back at the target, Delta finally declared the compound clear but we had little to show for it. As intelligence later confirmed, Aideed had been there but had avoided capture. He reportedly heard the helicopters as the assault force approached then managed to slip away in the darkness during the initial chaos of the helicopter assault. In spite of the disappointment, we knew the task force was keeping the pressure on, ruining Aideed's sleep, and that we were getting close.

As the task force dealt with the frustrations of tracking the elusive Somali warlord, the Rangers and operators continued to train and keep our skills sharp. One relatively rare training opportunity came in September when the task force FSO informed me a U.S. Navy ship would be arriving just off the coast in Mogadishu. In order to sharpen their skills at calling for naval gunfire, Ranger FOs were always looking for a chance to work with an actual U.S. Navy ship rather than just a simulator. Through headquarters channels, we contacted the vessel, which turned out to be the USS *Rentz*, a Navy fast frigate, which carried among its weapons a 5-inch gun. The crew of the *Rentz* gladly welcomed the opportunity and invited us to come aboard to discuss the training.

On the day that the USS *Rentz* appeared on the horizon near the Somali coast, taking up station just off Mogadishu, we prepared to visit the ship. The *Rentz* carried small Navy Seahawk helicopters and sent one to the airfield to pick up our small group on the airfield tarmac just outside our compound gate. Along with me, our small group included a major who was the fire support officer on the headquarters staff at Delta, and one or two others. After landing on the postage stamp-sized deck of the ship, we were received by the captain and crew. We took a brief tour of the ship, then went to the fire direction center for a short meeting to set up the training. While we could not call in live rounds from the ship's gun, we would get good experience talking to each other on the radio and working out procedures during simulated missions. After about an hour of informal discussions with the Navy crew we were invited to join the ship's captain for lunch. We filed into the small space of the officers' mess for a sit-down meal with plates and Navy silver service. After weeks of eating packaged Army rations, the Navy chow was an excellent change. The ship was like a small oasis of America in the middle of the vast blue ocean. Soon after lunch, we departed on one of the Navy Seahawk helicopters, which lifted off the small deck as the ship pitched in the ocean waves. It took us back to the airfield where I got off and headed to the hangar to brief my team of Ranger FOs. The next day, at the designated time, we set up radios on the roof of the TOC and called out the USS *Rentz*. Working with the Navy crew, we practiced calls for fire from the frigate's 5-inch guns. Even without firing live rounds, we got some good practice working through the Navy procedures. Better yet, the short trip out to the USS *Rentz* at sea had been a great break from the routine in the hangar and compound.

And so it went through the first couple of weeks in September. In addition to the Lig Ligato House and old Russian Compound missions, the task force also launched on a quick daytime raid when Rangers with 3rd Platoon, travelling in a resupply convoy near Mogadishu's New Port, thought they identified Aideed near a Somali police station. The assault force launched in the afternoon and fast-roped into the dusty street around the station. The target was quickly secured along with all the Somalis inside. The raid went smoothly with the exception that it had been a case of mistaken identity and the target was not our man.

As September wore on there were few, if any, more signs of Aideed and his trail seemed to be growing cold. In spite of this, outside of the airfield, the SNA resistance to the UN continued to grow, with almost daily enemy activity. Our surveillance aircraft frequently identified Aideed's SNA militia setting up roadblocks, as well as other similar hostile activity around the city. Growing restless, the task force itched to get at them. Based upon this increasing enemy activity, coupled with the need to pressure Aideed and facilitate the collection of intelligence, a major change was finally made. With approval from Washington, D.C., the commanders in the TOC ordered the net to be cast wider in the city. While Aideed would remain the primary target, the task force would also begin to take down his shadow government and capture its key leaders. This was an approach most of us had advocated and hoped for from the first development of our plans. However, up to this point in the mission, the policy of restraint from Washington had kept the focus narrowly on Aideed. Now the gloves were coming off to a greater degree and we began to reap the benefits of surprise on Aideed's lieutenants. But before we turned up the heat on the SNA leaders, there was another issue that had to be addressed.

Early on, during the very first raid on the Lig Ligato House, we had already experienced some of the complexities that characterized the UN coalition and its entanglements with the local Somalis. The coalition had many weaknesses and internal frictions. Its forces were composed, in large part, of military units from countries that had been longtime foes. Among these were the Greeks and Turks, and the Pakistanis and Indians. This was humorously brought home to us not long after the Indian brigade arrived in Mogadishu that fall.

One afternoon, we passed through the Indian Army sector as we made our way to the desert ranges for training. The Indian units were still getting settled and, naturally, we saw them digging in fighting positions for their armored vehicles in their assigned sector, orienting out to the west, away from the city. But we also noticed with surprise that just as many positions were being dug facing east, back toward the UN-controlled area. We casually asked the Indian officers about this and they explained, pointing toward the coalition area, "Yes, of course, because that's where the Pakistanis are." With the mix of languages, military equipment, and procedures, shifting focus within the coalition and running it smoothly was a challenge under the best of circumstances.

But there was more at work than normal frictions on the political front. We were well aware that Somalia had previously been a Soviet client state and, before that, it had been in the Italian colonial sphere. We also knew that our Italian allies still maintained close ties to the Somalis, along with ambitions for reestablishing their influence. The Italian network included ties to the Habr Gidr clan and, through them, continued contact with the SNA and their former colonial subject General Aideed. The Italian Army contingent was located at the north end of Mogadishu Airport. From this slightly elevated position, the Italian military units maintained a good view of our compound, to include the hangar and TOC. Our intelligence network within the task force continually monitored the Italians' contact with Aideed's group, but this had previously been overlooked and tolerated in the spirit of the coalition. However, not long after the task force had arrived and begun operations, we discovered that the Italians at the north end of the field were observing our activities and sending reports to Aideed. The Italians finally crossed the line when they attempted to provide the SNA early warning of the helicopter-borne force taking off for a mission. Accompanied by a section of gun trucks mounting their heavy weapons and a contingent of burly Delta operators, the commander and J2 intelligence officer paid a visit to the Italian TOC. The damning intelligence reports were laid on the table by the J2 and then our commander made the point in the "international language" that this would not be tolerated ever again. After that conference, Aideed received no more help from the UN forces. That said, more and more the U.S. military contingent was on its own in attempting to secure the city. Some of the various units of the UN coalition, especially those who had taken heavy casualties in the street fights with the SNA, cut local deals and maintained an uneasy status quo of "live and let live" with Aideed's militia.

Simultaneously, and unknown to us at the time, Aideed continued to skillfully attempt to counter our intelligence efforts. He even managed to clandestinely get a number of Habr Gidr clansmen and women inside the compound as contract workers. They gleaned what intelligence they could, as they swept floors and did laundry around the compound, then passed it on to Aideed. Meanwhile, we hoped our newly approved efforts to expand the pressure on Aideed's network would keep us one step ahead of Aideed and the SNA.

While Aideed remained elusive, his number two man in the Somali National Alliance, Osman Atto, was much more visible on an almost daily basis. A wealthy businessman and the public face of the SNA, Atto moved openly and often elaborately in expensive vehicles, in and around the Mogadishu neighborhoods. He owned numerous businesses and properties around Mogadishu where our intelligence assets often identified him during the day. While Atto was almost always guarded by the SNA militia, he did not go to any discernible lengths to conceal his movements.

On the afternoon of September 18, aerial surveillance of an automotive garage owned by Atto picked up a likely target, then confirmed his presence with "positive ID" at that location. The task force quickly saddled up in our small fleet of helicopters and launched a mission to capture him. The daytime insertion included Delta operators aboard the Little Birds landing in the open spaces inside the compound and Rangers fast-roping into the surrounding streets. There were not many tall buildings around the garage compound and the fast-rope was relatively easy from a low altitude. Once on the ground, I quickly found Captain Steele and we took up positions with the rest of the Rangers arrayed outside the metal and concrete walls of the compound. The raid went off smoothly and the garage was quickly secured as the few Somali militiamen on guard quickly scurried away before our assault. The compound and buildings were searched carefully but Atto had disappeared.

Many years later, as the fortunes of war shifted, a friend of mine returned to Mogadishu where Osman Atto was still a player in local politics. After being introduced to Atto, my friend got to know our wily former enemy. Atto took him to the garage and showed him the carefully hidden entrance to an escape tunnel under the office desk that he had used that day to evade the searching Delta operators.

While Atto had escaped the raid, we did find signs of SNA activity, to include a rival clan militiaman chained to a tree by his neck in the compound. He was one of the few Somalis in the neighborhood that day who were happy to see us when we stormed into the compound. As the assault force departed the neighborhood, walking the short distance to our pick-up site, we met no resistance and saw few Somalis in the streets. We moved about four blocks to an open space in the urban sprawl where Blackhawks cycled for the pickup, landing in a large intersection. The relatively simple operation, aided by daylight, had taken under one hour from initially hitting the ground until extraction.

In spite of this obvious warning that he was now in our gunsights, Osman Atto continued to move relatively openly and direct SNA operations around the city. Maintaining constant surveillance on Atto's known residence and offices from our high-tech reconnaissance aircraft bore fruit just a few days later.

On the afternoon of September 21, Atto was positively identified entering a small white sedan, accompanied by a single bodyguard who drove the car. The assault force launched but maintained a distant orbit, while the recon birds discreetly tracked Atto through the crowded streets. Looking ahead along the vehicle's route, the task force laid a trap on a relatively broad thoroughfare with just a few closely spaced buildings.

Demonstrating the flexibility of the assault template and value of the rehearsals, a portion of the Delta assault element was put on the ground after an AH-6 Little Bird stopped Atto's vehicle with a burst of warning shots into the road ahead of it. As the Delta assaulters stormed up to the vehicle, the driver brazenly came out of the car with his AK-47. He was immediately neutralized with a leg shot. This is another example of the relative restraint that characterized our approach to missions during that time. As the assaulters dealt with the driver, Atto fled into a nearby building. Assault teams began to secure and clear that and other nearby buildings, sorting through a number of Somalis they encountered inside. As the Delta assaulters questioned one of the Somali males, he confirmed he was, in fact, Osman Atto. As the Delta assault teams worked on the ground, Somalis in the nearby neighborhoods began to react and converge on the intersection where the action was occurring.

Flying above in Super 64 in my usual position, I had a ringside seat for this mission. After assessing the target and force requirements, the commanders had made the decision to put only a few Delta assault teams on the ground; most of the force, to include the rest of the Rangers and me, remained airborne, orbiting over the target area, watching the action unfold. We could clearly see crowds of Somalis gathering around the neighborhood. We also noted the burning tires that had been lit to help signal the SNA militia and vector them into the location of the raid. Aware of this on the ground, the assault force worked quickly.

Once he had been identified, Atto was flex-cuffed and quickly taken to the flat roof of the two-story building where he had been found. There, Cliff Wolcott and his copilot, Donovan Briley, brought Super 61 in, performing another feat of aerial maneuver. As I watched out the side of Super 64, I could see there was not enough clearance for the rotor blades to land the entire helicopter, but the pilots came on, easing the bird closer until the rotor blades were nearing the adjoining wall. They were just close enough now to set one wheel on the roof and balance Super 61 there in a half hover while Atto was loaded, before his Delta guards jumped on board. In accordance with our templated plan, if Super 61 had to depart, then our Blackhawk Super 64 would run in and replace it in orbit, providing support over the target.

As Super 61 flew away with the high-value prisoner, our aircraft Super 64 joined the action and our door gunners were keyed to engage targets. On the way in from our safe holding pattern and while we were over the target area, our pilots slalomed the aircraft up and down, bucking and weaving in order to present a more difficult target. Along with the steadily increasing ground fire, this made for a thrilling ride as we roared down closer to the rooftops then climbed steeply, soaring higher above the streets. Moving counter-clockwise in our circular orbit over the target area kept the action on our left side and continued to give me an excellent view all through the raid. From our position above, we could see a veritable hornet's nest of growing activity on the ground. We also observed one or two smoke trails in the air around us and heard the increasing crack of gunfire directed our way. Dense crowds were now beginning to converge as the Delta assaulters steadily collapsed their perimeter and methodically fell back inside the target building. The teams emerged in turn onto the rooftop for extraction by the helicopters. As they regrouped and were moving up to the roof, Somali gunmen began to probe the shrinking perimeter. Short, sharp exchanges took place, and the Delta snipers orbiting in Super 62 continued to engage gunmen in support of the extraction. With the Somalis effectively held at bay for the moment, the last of the assaulters reached the roof and climbed into a helicopter, which quickly lifted off. The task force reassembled in the air at a safer altitude and victoriously headed for the airfield.

Upon landing, the leaders quickly moved to the TOC and received news that Atto had been positively identified. This was a major score for Task Force Ranger, boosting our confidence and simultaneously increasing the pressure on Aideed. Later, I talked over the mission with John Breen and Jim Klingaman, who had both been in the TOC, observing the action on real-time video from the surveillance aircraft. They told me that our orbiting aircraft had been the target of not just a few, but over a score of RPGs, in addition to constant small-arms fire. While absorbing this news during the mission hotwash — standard procedure for all of the key leaders after a mission — we drew a number of lessons.

The first lesson was that we felt we had validated the template of the assault force and our approach to the raids. We also learned that time was absolutely critical. Based on our recent experiences, and especially after our observations of the mission to capture Atto, we understood that we could strike anywhere in the city, day or night, and the Somalis could not react fast enough to provide more than token resistance. Key to this success was to stay on a strict timeline, to get in and out. During daylight, this timeline equated to about an hour and was just a little longer at night. With their rudimentary but effective techniques, such as burning tires around the contact area, the Somalis would react to the raids by gathering in crowds and assembling the militia. They would then gradually move toward a raid site, such as they had done during our capture of Atto. However, they could not do this effectively in under an hour. We had more than enough combat power between the two platoons in the Ranger blocking positions, and the Ranger convoy, with its heavy crew, served weapons when they arrived. This force was enough to easily deal with anything the Somalis could throw at us, provided we stayed within the timeline. Anything beyond that could see the number of Somalis opposing us quickly grow to tens of thousands. We also reasoned that any issues which developed could be partially addressed by the fact that the UN should deploy their quick reaction force (QRF). This force would provide an infantry company from the 10th Mountain Division within 30 minutes and the remainder of the U.S. brigade within hours. Some of these conclusions would prove to be valid and others less solid as time went on. They were partially shaken just days later when a Blackhawk from the regular U.S. forces supporting the UN was hit by an RPG and shot down while patrolling over the city. Two of the crew members survived the crash but found themselves alone among the gathering Somalis. Fortunately, the crash had occurred not far from the neighborhood of a Somali clan friendly to the UN. The survivors were able to escape and evade the hostile Habr Gidr until they reached a nearby haven where a Somali family hid them until contact with the UN forces could be made. Therein lay one of the key problems. The 10th Mountain reaction force, which was tasked to be moving within minutes, was inexplicably delayed from reaching the crash site for almost two and a half hours. The other concern was that the Somalis had been able to effectively employ an RPG to shoot down a helicopter. Rocket-propelled grenades are designed to be anti-tank weapons, fired by a gunner on a flat trajectory. The backblast from the rocket could actually injure the man using the weapon if the rear of the launcher was angled toward the ground, which is what is required to take aim at a flying aircraft.

Based on our own experience that week during the Atto raid, we assumed the downed aircraft was the result of a lucky shot. What we did not know was that a shadowy Saudi extremist named Osama bin Laden, then based in nearby Sudan, had offered Aideed the assistance of his group, Al Qaeda, made up of Islamic terrorists. Some of the terrorists had been in the Afghan War against the Soviets and brought with them experience in modifying RPG launchers to enable them to be fired into the air. The shootdown of the U.S. helicopter was, in fact, the result of this Al Qaeda assistance.

However, we remained confident in the demonstrated effectiveness of our tactics and approach to the raids, as well as in our 160th pilots and aircraft. By all accounts, our raids were increasing the pressure on Aideed, and the effectiveness of our intelligence efforts grew by the day. Although the capture of Atto was our last mission in September, the task force continued to receive numerous intelligence reports with potential opportunities to capture Aideed or more of his lieutenants.

The pace of mission planning and spinning up for potential operations or "optempo" remained high. Frequently, over the next few days and nights, the assault force would be alerted and begin the process of loading the aircraft and preparing to launch, only to get the "stand down" order. As the calendar changed to October, we experienced this three times in a 36-hour period, leaving us short of sleep and our patience worn.

That first weekend in October brought us some relief from the intensive schedule we had followed since we arrived. On Saturday, much of the task force had participated in a group run around the airfield, along the dirt road inside the UN perimeter. We broke into ability groups based on our own speed and did a staggered start. Cliff Wolcott, the lead pilot in Super 61, helped orchestrate the run and joked with those of us who didn't join the "fast group" up front. As the groups took off and began to space out, I found myself running alongside my pilot Mike Durant. Mike and I weren't out to set any records and talked of home and the missions while we ran.

Later that day, the task force had a rare meal of fresh meat provided by some of the Delta snipers who had practiced their skills on some wild African boar. Dan Busch was one of the Delta snipers and a favorite among B Company. Dan had served as a Ranger in B Company prior to going to Delta selection. He would often come over to our area, sit on a cot, and talk with my bunkmate, First Sergeant Glenn Harris. I liked Dan and was drawn to his positive attitude. He said it came from our shared Christian faith. He had told his mother not to worry about him because he was "just one click from heaven."

Glenn Harris was another fast friend I made in the company. A solid and serious Ranger first sergeant, he was friendly and always positive when I dealt with him one-on-one. Glenn never treated me like an outsider to the company. Glenn and I, along with Dan Busch, spent time talking on our cots in the small area designated for senior leaders in B Company, which also included Captain Mike Steele and our executive officer, Lee Ryswyk. Glenn would return home from Mogadishu only to die the following year in a training accident at Fort Benning when his parachute carried him away from the airfield drop zone and into a swollen river where he was lost.

As the weekend continued, another highlight for the Rangers came when the TOC set up a schedule for us to call back to the U.S. We did this on a single shared telephone line, connecting back to the 3rd Battalion headquarters at Fort Benning where our wives were lined up, waiting their turn to talk. The schedule was spaced out over a couple of days to give everyone a chance and my turn came on Saturday night. I was the second to last on the schedule, followed by an anxious Ranger, Sergeant Casey Joyce. We were given exactly five minutes to talk and Casey kept sticking his head in the room to see if I was finished yet. I heard Beth's voice for the first time in almost two months and got updates on the baby. Finally, Casey pressed into the room and I handed off the phone as his wife Deanna took the receiver from Beth back in Georgia. Along with events to boost our morale, like the phone calls and "fun run," there were still three "spin ups" and false alerts for the assault force over that weekend. Yet, it had been a good couple of days and now we looked forward to relaxing a little on Sunday.

6

Into the Valley

War means fightin' and fightin' means killin'.
Nathan Bedford Forrest

While we were always postured and standing by to respond
to an alert, on Sunday, October 3, the commanders gave
us a break from the intensive training and daily signature
flights. That morning, I went with Mike Steele, Larry
Perino, and some others to a small beach among the rocks
across the airfield from our hangar. The surf was rough,
but we cooled off for a few minutes before deciding to
head back to the compound. Mike wanted to stay and
aggressively dove into the surf, swimming out deeper into
the rough waters. Since there were numerous UN soldiers
and some other Rangers still on the beach, the rest of us
left him there and headed back to our compound. Later
on, I had a plan to infiltrate the white trailers where the
pilots were billeted as they had normal bathrooms and
porcelain. This was a luxury, as opposed to having to use
the sweltering plastic Portalet boxes placed along the outer
wire of our compound.

A few hours after we had returned from the beach, as I walked by the medical unit next to our hangar, I overheard one of the Air Force medics say they were looking for blood donors because there had been a shark attack at the beach. I had not seen Captain Steele since I had been back and I did not realize that he had been called to the TOC. Worrying over my boss as I continued my way toward the white trailers, I soon learned that it was a soldier from the 10th Mountain who had been attacked, just off the beach, by a hammerhead shark. In spite of the intensive efforts and numerous blood transfusions used to try to save him, the soldier had died.

I continued on and successfully made it into the trailers, completing my mission. Then, a short time later, while walking back to the front of the hangar, I saw a flurry of activity around the TOC. I knew this meant a "spin up" and that I was already late for the mission brief. Hurrying into the TOC, I found the key leaders grouped around the dry erase board and watching the real-time surveillance video on the screen mounted above and to the left. Jim Klingaman was beginning his sketch diagram of a group of large buildings. As we watched, the reconnaissance helicopters or "recce birds" tracked a white sedan moving through crowded neighborhoods. Simultaneously, a staff officer gave us an intelligence update. According to the intelligence, a group of Aideed's top leaders were meeting near the Olympic Hotel in the vast Bakara Market in the center of the Habr Gidr territory. However, the Somali spy providing the information did not believe that Aideed was present. Sunday is the first day of the work week in Islamic countries and the market was crowded. The intel brief recounted that we had a report on the meeting from a new source and that spy was now driving the white sedan. The plan was for the spy to use it to pinpoint the target building for us. As we waited tensely, the commanders tried to direct the driver with long, awkward delays over the radio via the task force interpreter speaking Somali. When it finally seemed that the car was stopped at the correct location, Jim Klingaman began the details of his sketch.

The intelligence rep continued on with the brief, noting that our surveillance assets had observed a relatively large, heavily armed group of about 30 militiamen guarding the building, along with other obvious security precautions. Other significant portions of the SNA militia were nearby, all around the Bakara Market, which also contained a large arms bazaar piled with weapons and ammunition. Another significant report was that a group of about 400 militiamen, who had been previously sent to Sudan to train with Al Qaeda at the invitation of Osama bin Laden, had recently returned to Mogadishu. These 400 newly trained fighters were now set up in the Sheik Aden Adeere compound, not far from the Bakara Market. All of this information warranted our professional consideration but did not overly concern or intimidate us. We had faith in our plan, knew our time limitations, and were taking over 200 of the best fighters in the world. We also knew the 160th would be overhead.

As the briefing went on, standing off to the side consulting with Colonel Boykin, Major General Garrison weighed the risks. He, too, realized the dangers but shared our faith in the plan and this was too lucrative a target to pass up. While this new Somali intelligence source seemed somewhat tentative, the information he provided added up. The decision was made to launch. As the intelligence rep concluded his brief and made his last comments, the leaders began to move toward the door. I noted the heavy Somali security element again and moved over to Colonel Boykin to ask if we would go in heavy by getting rockets on the AH-6s today. He looked at me deliberately and answered, "Yes Jim, you are getting the rockets."

The hangar soon echoed with the orders to "Get it on" and the chalks moved out quickly through the mid-afternoon heat. On my way out of the cavernous hangar entrance, I saw our company executive officer, Lieutenant Lee Ryswyk. Jaded by the spate of spin ups and scratches, I told him to wait for me as we would be back in a few minutes and "we'll go to chow." Upon reaching Super 64, we loaded on as usual, then sat sweating for a few minutes with the helicopter rotor blades turning. Soon, we received the disappointing, but predictable, call for everyone to unload, but, as we climbed out of the helicopters, another call came for key leaders to return to the TOC. As I walked back into the TOC alongside Captain Steele and chalk leader Larry

Perino, we found the commanders glued to the screen and
Jim Klingaman working feverishly on the board to modify
the sketch.

Because of all the security, the Somali spy had been
afraid to drive down to the actual meeting location and
had parked a block away. After this had been awkwardly
established over the radio through the interpreter, Major
General Garrison had forcefully directed the spy to drive
down to the target building, ordering him to stop there and
put his hood up, feigning engine trouble. This exchange
had begun as we were loading the aircraft. Now, as we
reassembled in the cramped TOC spaces, the white car —
distinguishable by a cross taped on the hood — could be
seen on the video screen just coming to a halt in front of a
multi-story building. After a minute or two of hesitation
and milling around outside the vehicle, we saw the Somali
driver clearly raise the vehicle's hood: confirmation.
Jim Klingaman modified his sketch to the new building,
quick adjustments were made to our plan, and, almost
immediately, we were moving back to the aircraft.
Although there was significant and growing promise with
this target, we had been through this stop-and-start process
numerous times in the past weeks. Hurrying back to Super
64, I climbed back in and squeezed into place, packed in
among the other Rangers, and waited. As I got settled, I
looked out the right side of the aircraft and noticed Bill
Garrison moving among the birds. He had walked out of
the TOC with the assault force and was now shaking hands

and giving encouragement to the operators, Rangers, and pilots as they saddled up in the aircraft. It struck me that he had never done this before. The assault force was soon reloaded and set aboard the aircraft. I now had my radio headset on, keyed to the UHF channel designated for fire support. In order to keep the radio traffic down to a minimum, key events were often called using individual codewords. As I listened to the static, the calm voice of one of the pilots suddenly broke in, "Irene, Irene, Irene" – codeword for launch. Reacting almost in surprise, the helicopters hesitated a moment, then quickly revved their engines and surged into the air, heading west. We initially flew out over the ocean, heading briefly down the coast, then began a long slow curve back in toward the city. In the tradition of warriors for thousands of years, we would keep the afternoon sun at our backs for as long as possible to help screen our approach. It was not a long flight, even with our route out to the west.

As the task force headed over the city and approached the target area, it turned again to the right, into the wind and lining up a north-to-south approach. Our Ranger Blackhawks, still high above the rooftops, slowed their pace, allowing the birds with the Delta assault element to get in and clear the target. The streets were just wide enough around the multi-story target building to allow the MH-6 Little Birds to weave in and drop off their assaulters while the two big Blackhawks quickly inserted theirs as well. The initial wave of helicopters carrying the Delta operators immediately kicked up a blowing storm of dust, causing the trail MH-6 to lose his precise bearing on the street and abort the landing, peeling off to the west in a "go around." Outside the billowing cloud of dust, the MH-6 pilot found a relatively clear intersection about two blocks away and landed. The team of Delta assaulters jumped off, quickly getting their bearings, and moved toward the target building even as the other teams, already there ahead of them, stormed over the walls, throwing "flash bang" stun grenades and breaching the gates.

As the first wave of helicopters cleared the area, the four Ranger Blackhawks continued to come in slowly toward the target, trying to remain steady and allow the billowing dust to clear. Super 64 seemed to inch forward, still high above the rooftops, as the pilots struggled to keep stability. Finally, we realized our Blackhawks were just renewing the milky, churning storm. It was obvious they could not get lower. When the order was shouted for "ropes out," there was another delay as one of the long thick green ropes got hung up in a telephone wire. As the pilots jockeyed the bird forward to untangle it, Crew Chief Bill Cleveland leaned forward, out over his minigun, then finally called the rope clear and on the ground. We still seemed too high, far above the rooftops as the aircraft began to hover in the cloud. Over the engine noise we suddenly heard "Go, Go, Go!" but the Rangers in the doorways hesitated for a brief second as we seemed far too high. Then, the orchestrated surge began. As I pressed forward in sequence, I watched the Rangers slide down, instantly disappearing into the cloud of milky brown. As the aircraft rotors thundered in my ears, I could see the rope swaying in front of me, just far enough out that I had to commit my body weight to reach it. As I jumped, I felt the thick rope set into the palms of my gloves, then I jerked it against my body, catching my weight while trying to lock my boots onto it. Instantly, as my weight hit the rope, I plummeted down into the silty cloud. The friction of the rope burned and began to sear my hands as the fall continued, going on and on until I finally crashed into the street. The aircraft was still creeping slightly forward, but that helped us as, otherwise, we would have dangerously "dog piled" on top of each other. I took a few disoriented steps, slamming into a wall before getting my bearings.

Amid the swirling dust and thunder of the helicopter above me, I heard another sound – sustained gunfire. As the Rangers around me on the south corners of the target building began to sort themselves out, it was obvious that those to the north were already in contact with the enemy. As the firefight began to build, sporadic gunfire could be heard, answered by the heavier automatic weapons of the Rangers. As the last of the Rangers hit the ground, the crew chiefs in the Blackhawks above us cut the ropes away. The ropes dropped to the street with a rippling crash before the big green aircraft peeled off to a safe orbit as we consolidated our perimeter around the target building. As the dust began to settle and the contact to the north went on, we could also hear the sounds of the Delta assaulters continuing to breach and clear rooms inside the target building.

The ragged Somali security force that had initially been hanging around the target building had scattered at the approach of the task force. But a few of the gunmen had hung back and fired at the Rangers on the north side, initiating the firefight that we could hear in that direction. However, our perimeter was quickly being established and the immediate area brought under control as the Ranger blocking positions tied in to each other and formed a shield around the Delta assaulters clearing the building. I did my normal check-ins on the radio, ensuring I had good comms with my forward observers and with Super 61. The two designated Blackhawks were now vigilantly orbiting overhead carrying the Delta snipers. I checked in using my radio call sign: "Super 61, this is Juliette 36, radio check, over." The pilot, Cliff Wolcott, answered that he could read me "loud and clear" and was in position, with the snipers scanning and ready to receive our requests.

All around me, the Rangers at R1 on the southeast Ranger blocking position were set, facing outwards amid the tight alleys and debris of the narrow street. Captain Steele and his radio operator, along with the Air Force CCT sergeant, clustered by a telephone pole a few feet behind me. My forward observer at R1, Sergeant Mike Goodale, crouched nearby with another Ranger, behind a wrecked car that was backed up close to the target building. Goodale had been raised in the B Company fire support team, beginning as a young private, straight out of initial training. After three-plus years with B Company, he was now a veteran Ranger. He had mastered the skills of being a Ranger forward observer and wasn't afraid to give his opinion or suggest another way of doing business. There had always been a strong rivalry between the fire support teams of Alpha and Bravo companies. When I had come on board at the last minute with B Company, Mike and his best friend and fellow forward observer Raleigh Cash had jealously guarded the standard practices of their team. But Mike always had a smile on his face and I had heard him talk in the hangar about his girlfriend, Kira, and how serious they were. He was absolutely trustworthy as a Ranger and forward observer. After working together on the train-up at Fort Bragg and the previous missions in Mogadishu, we had now formed a solid team.

Seeing Sergeant Goodale crouched behind the crushed car in our blocking position, looking out to his front, I knew that sector was covered. As I scanned the rest of the perimeter around me, I took a moment and quickly reached down into the cargo pocket on the side of my desert camouflage pants leg, pulling out the disposable Kodak camera I carried on every mission. I briefly lined up as much of the Ranger position as I could, then centered on the target building with Mike Goodale and Ranger Mike Kurth in the foreground, before snapping off a picture. It would become the only picture taken on the ground that day. Turning around and away from the target building,

I moved a few steps forward in the perimeter with some Rangers covering the long street running east away from the target building. One of the squad leaders, Staff Sergeant Kenny Boorn, a hulking warrior like his Viking ancestors, was across the street against the wall with Corporal Jamie Smith close by on his flank. Tall, lanky Specialist Carlos Rodriguez, who was just 18 years old, knelt in front of me, covering the street on our side. There were small groups of Rangers similarly positioned in the alleyways around us. Back behind me further to the west, I could see Sergeant First Class Sean Watson, the team leader at R4, directing his Rangers. I did not have visual contact with the Rangers at the R2 position to the north, but confirmed I had comms with my forward observer at that position by checking in with Specialist Joe Thomas on the radio. Similarly, Sergeant Jeff McLaughlin at R3 on the other side of the target building to the northwest, and Private First Class Jeff Young at R4 next to us to the west, checked in on the radio as they covered those positions.

While Delta continued to clear the building and the Rangers held our blocking positions, there was various activity involving Somalis around us. One old man had been caught on the street near the target building walking home from the store. He sat patiently on a curb not far from Sergeant Boorn, with his bags alongside, waiting for the tumult to end. We were not in heavy contact now, but were being targeted by individual gunmen lurking in the windows of the buildings and on the streets around us, taking occasional pot shots. At the R4 position next to us on the southwest corner, one gunman persisted. Hiding behind a large metal shed about 150 yards away, he continued to pop up and fire into the Ranger position. Sean Watson ended this annoyance in a small mushroom cloud with a shot from a light anti-tank rocket that had been carried in by his Rangers. On our corner at R1, we began to receive similar harassment fire. The Rangers under Sergeant Boorn dueled back and forth with the Somalis using well-aimed shots and controlled bursts of fire. In the middle of this exchange, a Somali woman walked across the intersection in front of our position, seemingly oblivious to the firefight. She casually raised her hands in a "don't shoot" manner, but then began gesturing and pointing toward our location. It became clear, as the Somali militia probed forward through the maze of streets, they were not exactly sure of our positions and locations. Somali non-combatants, such as this woman, began to try to infiltrate our positions and assist the gunmen. Behind me, where Mike Goodale was crouched behind the wrecked car, the Rangers let off a short fusillade of fire toward the southern approach, cutting down other probing gunmen. These unfortunate Somalis had been searching for the contact area and blundered into our perimeter.

About the same time, a call came from Specialist Joe Thomas, my forward observer at R2, to the northeast of the target building. He was receiving fire from Somali gunmen east of his position and requested assistance from the snipers on Super 61. I immediately passed him off to pilot Cliff Wolcott, and continued to monitor the duel to my front. Soon, Super 61 slewed through the air above us, fruitlessly searching for the enemy. After a few passes, I added my request, "61, this is Juliette 36, receiving fire at R1 about 150 to 200 meters directly east of our position," asking that the snipers scan in that area. After a few more passes, the gunfire on our end largely ceased and things momentarily calmed down. I told Cliff, "End of mission," releasing him to return to his safe orbit. Behind me, Mike Steele called that the target building was secure. The Delta assaulters had captured a number of key targets and were now bringing them down to the street. These were all good signs that the mission was proceeding on track. Further, the Ranger convoy had arrived with its HMMVs and 5-ton trucks, speeding through R4 and Sean Watson's position to marshal on the north side of the target. In the middle of the various radio traffic on the mission's progress and coordinating efforts with my forward observers, another call was heard. We had one Ranger seriously injured on the north side.

On the insertion, as the pilots struggled to keep the aircraft stable, Private First Class Todd Blackburn had missed the swaying fast-rope and fallen approximately 90 feet to the street. The chalk leader there at R3 in the northwest, Sergeant Matt Eversmann, had his hands full, working to move the unconscious Blackburn to a safe position, coordinate medical attention, and deal with the contact going on around his blocking position. Delta medics had moved out to R3 from the target building to assist and now continued to work on Blackburn. Sergeant First Class Bart Bullock, a hulking dark-haired Delta assaulter and medic, assessed the 18-year-old Ranger's injuries as life-threatening.

When the convoy arrived amidst the continuing fire, Bullock and Eversmann approached the vehicles and talked to the commander, Lieutenant Colonel McKnight, requesting to immediately evacuate Blackburn. McKnight consulted with the mission commander, Gary Harrell, and his aviation counterpart, Tom Matthews, who was orbiting above in the command and control aircraft. With limited landing space options and the gradually increasing contact at the blocking positions, a helicopter evacuation was ruled out. McKnight felt he had enough vehicles in the convoy to cut three loose and send them back to the airfield with the stricken Ranger. McKnight hurried over to Staff Sergeant Jeff Struecker, who was leading a squad of Rangers in the convoy and personally driving one of the HMMVs himself. The battalion commander gave Struecker his new tasking, directing the Rangers to quickly load Blackburn aboard. As Struecker's trio of HMMVs peeled out of the convoy and sped away, they turned south and passed in a cloud of dust in front of our position at R1. The Rangers in the perimeter had not received any updates on these events and were surprised to see the vehicles race away from the target. In the confusion, some of the Rangers mistakenly believed

Struecker's team was turning away from the growing contact and abandoning us. But as Struecker drove through the Habr Gidr neighborhoods, racing for the airfield, he would have other problems to deal with.

All along the route of the three HMMVs working their way through the Habr Gidr neighborhoods, the Somalis were beginning to assemble and react en masse. The appearance of the U.S. vehicles in their midst drew hails of gunfire from buildings and alleyways along the route. The machine gunners in the turrets of the HMMVs were firing constantly now, slewing their guns around to hammer windows and alleyways. Specialist Dominic Pilla, a tall, boisterous Ranger from New Jersey, manned an M240 machine gun in the back of Struecker's truck. He swung the machine gun toward a Somali militiaman approaching from an alley. They fired simultaneously and the gunman dropped to the street, but Pilla also fell to the floor of the HMMV. He had been killed instantly by an AK-47 round to the head. The small convoy sped on, firing nonstop but being shredded by fire from the neighborhoods. What seemed like a lifetime later, Struecker drove his bloody and bullet-scarred vehicles through the gates of the airfield, moving directly to the Task Force Ranger compound.

Meanwhile, back in my position at R1, Cliff Wolcott called me to say he was coming back in over our position to take one more look for the Somali gunmen who had been harassing us. I watched the Blackhawk come in low about two blocks out, as it turned to scan the streets. When Super

61 passed in front of me, I briefly turned away and, as I looked back, I heard a muffled bang and metal grinding as the aircraft began to slew and twist unnaturally. Trying to process what I was seeing, I initially tried to reason that Cliff was turning hard for a shot but, in reality, I felt doom. As the aircraft spun, I caught a glimpse of Cliff and his copilot Donovan Briley through the windshield, fighting to maintain control, then someone in the back of the bird lurching forward. Super 61 spun off to my left and out of sight to the north. Seconds later, I heard the ominous crunch of impact. The calls began to reverberate across the radio net: "61 is down, we have a Blackhawk down." Absorbing this shocking turn, Captain Steele began to coordinate with Lieutenant Tom DiTomasso up at R2, while we simultaneously continued preparations to load the convoy and depart. As the call came in that Delta was loading the prisoners, we began to anticipate the next move and started to collapse the Ranger perimeter. Steele now directed Lieutenant DiTomasso to take part of his group and move toward the crash site, which Tom had just observed about four blocks away, east of the R2 position.

At the crash site, incredibly, some survivors climbed out of the wreckage. The pilots had heroically kept the aircraft in a flat spin, but it had slammed down onto a wall and crashed forward, killing them both. The aircraft had maintained just enough stability, however, to allow the two crew chiefs and Delta snipers in the back to survive. One of the survivors was Dan Busch, who could be seen by the helicopters orbiting above, climbing out of the wreckage and going immediately back into the fight. Dan took up a position on a nearby corner and held off the approaching Somalis until a burst of AK-47 fire struck him in the stomach, just beneath his bulletproof protective plate. Jim Smith, another Delta sniper, pulled Dan back from the corner and tried to give him medical aid. Dan had been hit hard with a very serious stomach wound and would need immediate medevac. At this point, as the Somalis were still massing chaotically, one of the MH-6 Little Birds, which had earlier carried the Delta assaulters in on its two external bench seats, flew back in to try to save Dan. The MH-6 pilot, Chief Karl Maier, made an amazing landing among the hanging wires, rubble, and wreckage of Super 61. Finding a tight flat space on a street corner, Maier set the Little Bird down. He then held the aircraft controls with one hand and fired his MP5 submachine gun out his side door at approaching Somali gunmen with the other. Maier provided cover fire while his copilot helped Delta operator Jim Smith load the wounded Dan Busch onto one of the external benches. As Maier continued to fire his submachine gun, he was suddenly shocked to see Lieutenant DiTomasso run around a corner, and almost shot him. As AK-47 rounds impacted all around, the MH-6 lifted off like a Valkyrie, taking the mortally wounded Delta operator out of the firefight. Despite having just survived the crash with a serious gash in his face, Jim Smith refused to get on board and remained behind to help hold the position.

Almost immediately following the MH-6 taking off with Dan Busch, Super 68 – the Blackhawk with the Combat Rescue team – arrived, swooping in over the crash.

When the call came that Super 61 was down, a number of pieces in the contingency plans were ordered into play. In addition to Super 64 coming in to replace 61 in the orbit over the target area, the Combat Rescue team, to include my FO Butch Galliete, was called in. With the intensity of the battle around the crash site growing, the pilot Dan Jollota held the aircraft steady as the team began to fast-rope in. Suddenly, an RPG slammed into the vulnerable, hovering aircraft, and the onboard systems registered a catastrophic hit. The team was only about halfway complete in their exit and still on the ropes as Dan continued to hover with nerves of steel until they were all down. He was then able to nurse the stricken Blackhawk back over to the airfield a few miles away, crashing just inside the perimeter fence. Dan and his crew raced away from the badly damaged aircraft and fired up one of the spare Blackhawk helicopters on the ramp, immediately returning to the fight.

The Al Qaeda-trained RPG gunners who were firing at our helicopters that day had been part of the large group of Aideed's militia that had just returned from Sudan. Osama bin Laden and his shadowy Al Qaeda terrorist movement were currently based there, just to the north of Somalia. Earlier that summer, Bin Laden had offered his assistance to the SNA and that had resulted in a number of Aideed's fighters travelling to Sudan for a training course led by Bin

Laden and other veterans of the Afghan War against the Soviets. The Somalis had just completed their training and returned to Mogadishu, setting up a barracks in a facility owned by Sheik Aden Adeere, an Aideed supporter. Our intelligence section with Task Force Ranger had much of this information, and we kept close surveillance on the compound and fighters. Most of these newly returned militiamen were now rushing toward the action around the crash site. Some, with the assistance of their Al Qaeda advisors, were engaging our helicopters with RPGs.

As each member of the Combat Rescue team came off the fast ropes, they immediately went into action in the firefight around the aircraft wreckage. The team leader, Ranger Sergeant Al Lamb, began to direct some of his men into the fighting with the Somali militiamen, while others began to remove the wounded and the dead from the wreck. The USAF Pararescuemen (PJs) on the Combat Rescue team were specially trained experts on aircraft crash sites. While some of the Rangers on the team helped the PJs, others helped clear buildings and fought to hold back the increasing Somali attacks. As the Somali militia began to close on the crash site, the fighting closed to within a grenade's throw. A Russian grenade thrown by the Somalis soon landed in the wreck of Super 61 but failed to explode. Then some Rangers returned the gesture, throwing two of their own grenades over the nearby alley walls. This was followed by a single muffled explosion, and seconds later one of the U.S. M85 fragmentation grenades was tossed back. The American soldier had forgotten to pull the pin and the grenade was returned, this time exploding. While this was going on and the firefight around the crash site grew in intensity my FO Sergeant Galliete linked up with the previously injured Delta operator Jim Smith. In spite of his injuries from the crash, Smith was still in the fight and together they secured a narrow space of wall alongside the wreck of the Super 61. One of the few Rangers not to be wounded during the battle, Butch Galliete would spend the night shifting between critical points fighting in the defense of the crash site. As the assault force fought to establish a perimeter, the battle was now reaching a crescendo.

7

Storm of Steel

If your officer's dead and the sergeants look white,
Remember it's ruin to run from a fight:
So take open order, lie down, and sit tight,
And wait for supports like a soldier.
Wait, wait, wait like a soldier.
Rudyard Kipling, "The Young British Soldier"

While the Combat Rescue team was fast-roping onto the crash site, back at the target building I watched the Delta assaulters coming out of the gate and into the street. They loaded the prisoners on the 5-ton trucks as the Ranger convoy prepared to move, and we began collapsing the perimeter around the target building. Then a new order came down from the command aircraft over the radio net to the assault force on the ground. Along with the Combat Rescue team now fighting to secure the crash site and Lieutenant DiTomasso's group moving in that direction, the remainder of the assault force would consolidate in the street and move by foot to secure the area around the crash. At the same time, while this combined group of Rangers and Delta operators moved east, taking the most direct route, the convoy with its HMMVs and 5-ton trucks would also attempt to reach the crash site. However, the convoy would be unable to move with the assault force moving by foot, as the vehicles could not pass through the same narrow, debris-choked streets. The convoy would be forced to move separately along the wider main thoroughfares, trying to reach the crash site just a few blocks away.

I looked down at the Seiko diver's watch strapped to my wrist. The luminous dial showed 1630 hours and I realized we had been on the ground for nearly an hour. The world began to tilt now, out of the rehearsed sequence of the plan and registering the shock of contact with the enemy. Almost immediately, the assault force of Rangers and Delta operators began pushing east along the narrow streets. My stomach was in a cold knot now as I moved alongside Captain Steele. I knew the chances of survival were slim for the crew of the crashed helicopter. I also knew that somewhere ahead of us, blocks away, along with the handful of others on the Combat Rescue team, Butch Galliete was now on the ground at the crash site.

As we advanced, each one of us could see that all around us the Somalis were coming. Every second, resistance and enemy fire began to increase. The cracks of the Somali rifle fire were constant now, overhead and around us. The Somalis were massing and we could see the crowds, still blocks away but beginning to surge toward us. Aideed's militiamen aggressively moved through the alleys around

200

us and along the walls, firing and rapidly closing. They were reinforced by men and boys from the neighborhoods, joining in and carrying their AK-47 rifles. Rushing forward through the increasing fire, the assault force quickly covered two blocks then turned left. We headed north toward the crash site, still a few hundred meters away and beyond our vision but directly ahead.

As we turned the corner and began to move north, we became awash in combat. Bullets zipped along the walls around us and cracked incessantly overhead. Dust rose as Somali gunmen fired and ducked behind cover or were cut down by the Americans. Now, as the firefight began to rage, there was no hesitation over the rules of engagement. At the same time that we closed with the attacking Somalis, our column remained spread back toward the target building. It bogged down to a stop when the fight erupted in earnest all around us. The Rangers and operators in the assault force were taking cover, firing and maneuvering against the numerous attacking Somalis streaming into the streets.

At this point, the small-unit training and leadership of the Rangers and special operators began to play a critical role. For each small group of Rangers, their world became centered on the street corner or alleyway in front of them. The fighting narrowed down through tunnel vision to just a few meters. In this type of combat situation, soldiers are forced to focus on the fight immediately around them. At the same time, they also know that the battle is raging well beyond their small piece of ground and the enemy is out there, closing in. They have to trust the men to their left and right, knowing they are standing fast and will not break, just as they are doing for their comrades. As in a Spartan shield wall, survival comes from not only holding the enemy to your front but dependence on the men around you. To take a step back or falter and leave the man beside you exposed is inconceivable. As the chaos raged through the dusty streets and each Ranger and Delta operator fought to survive, I had absolute faith in the men around me. To my front and right were Delta operators along with the Rangers of Chalks One and Two; close behind coming up on my left and rear were the Rangers of Chalk Three under the command of Sergeant First Class Sean Watson.

I continued forward in the middle of the street alongside Captain Steele and his radio operator. As I advanced, I came across a wounded Ranger lying on his side in the road, immediately in front of me. I was surprised to look down into the face of one of my forward observers, Sergeant Mike Goodale. He had taken an AK-47 round through the hip and was in pain but seemed more surprised and frustrated at being hit than anything else. Without pausing, fixated on pushing forward to the crash site, I stepped over him and kept moving, knowing that a medic behind me would patch him up. To this day, I think back on that moment with waves of guilt but also knowing it was the tactically correct decision to not stop and help him.

The fighting continued and grew in intensity as the assault force began to move forward relentlessly. Nothing was going to stop us from reaching our comrades at the crash site. All around me, Rangers were rushing forward to cover, fighting to clear their corners, throwing grenades or hammering down alleys with automatic weapons. I watched one Ranger just ahead of me toss a grenade high in the air over the wall of a small corner compound just off to my left front. The grenade went off with a slightly muffled boom, then black smoke and dust rose from behind the walls of the compound. The heavy Somali fire coming down the streets caused the assault force to take cover in small groups as we tried to push forward. The Somali fire was answered thunderously by Rangers with M240 machine guns and rapid-firing squad automatic weapons.

Behind me guarding the rear of the column, Watson directed his teams fighting to hold back the growing waves of Somalis. Watson's Rangers fought from positions along the street while they anxiously waited for the rest of the column in front of them to move forward. His machine-gun teams roared almost continually now as he calmly directed their fire, conserving precious ammunition when possible.

Sean Watson was an old-school Ranger and "plank holder," meaning as a young private he had joined 3rd Battalion when it was originally formed in 1984. Now, he was the consummate Ranger platoon sergeant, with a strong personality and sarcastic dry wit that was legendary in Bravo Company. He was the driving force behind his Ranger platoon, and his calm but forceful leadership was now holding them together in the dusty streets as the battle grew in intensity.

One of Watson's machine gunners, Pete Neathery, was firing from a good position while covering the streets in front of him when an AK-47 round suddenly tore through his arm. Almost simultaneously, "Doc" Strous, the Ranger platoon medic with Chalk Three, was also hit by a round. Fortunately, the bullet struck one of the smoke grenades Strous was carrying, setting it off in a small explosion and engulfing him in a cloud of white. Strous emerged from the smoke and debris with his uniform and equipment badly torn. Otherwise uninjured, he immediately rushed across the street to Neathery. The incoming Somali fire cracked all around Strous as he dragged the wounded Ranger to a safer position and went to work on his mangled arm. From a position nearby, Sergeant Keni Thomas continued to provide covering fire, while Doc Strous struggled to control the bleeding from Neathery's shattered arm. Neathery was in intense pain and knew it was bad. Not wanting to see the gaping wound, he looked away and thought about his young wife and baby.

Around Watson's Rangers, shooting down the streets and pouring fire from the upper stories of the surrounding buildings, the Somalis continued to hammer into the column of Americans. Across the street from Watson, Sergeant Keni Thomas fired at the darting Somali gunmen while throwing hand grenades over the walls around his position. He directed one of the Rangers in his squad, Private Eric Suranski, to take out some Somali gunmen in the upper floors of a building down one of the nearby streets. Thomas pointed out the Somali position and Suranski slammed a 40mm round into the M203 grenade launcher attached to the bottom of his M4 rifle. He then quickly slid around the corner in front of him, looked across the top of the weapon, and sighted reflexively on the target for a fraction of a second. The Ranger immediately pulled the trigger then rocked back with the recoil of the heavy shotgun-like round. The high-explosive fragmentation grenade smoothly arced into the upper floor of the building to their front, taking out the Somali position in an explosion of gray and black smoke. Adding to their fire from machine guns, rifles, and grenade launchers, the Rangers began to use their light anti-tank rockets on the Somali positions. These light, high-explosive rockets came in a collapsible tube about the size of a man's arm. A handful of the rockets had been carried in on the assault, strapped to the backs of some of the Rangers. As Sergeant Watson's men began to fire their rockets, the rounds crisscrossed through the air with Russian-made RPGs fired by the Somalis. As the projectiles impacted on both sides, geysers of fire and dust began to erupt, adding to the chaos amid the now constant machine-gun and rifle fire.

As the rear of the column under Watson held fast, the Delta assaulters up front continued working their way forward. They moved tightly spaced in their teams of four, which was normal practice inside buildings clearing rooms and hallways. Near the middle of the column, Captain Steele, moving alongside his radio operator, paused a few paces away from me and yelled over the growing din into the hand mic of the radio. Just to Steele's left, I took a knee and scanned a debris-strewn berm down the street about 100 yards to our front. A Somali jumped up and ran forward, then dove back down behind a dirt berm for cover. In my mind I was confused by this strange behavior, but my training automatically kicked in. I was firing into the berm before I consciously realized that the Somali gunman was firing and maneuvering against us. Close beside me, Captain Steele bellowed that he could not hear the radio with me firing. In response I moved up a few steps just behind a team of Delta assaulters working their way forward along the wall to our right. Suddenly, they began to jerk and twist like they were being stung by bees as bullets ripped along the wall. The assaulter in the lead, jovial and friendly Earl Fillmore, dropped forward and hit the ground with dead weight. Fillmore and the rest of the Delta assaulters wore black plastic hockey helmets rather than the heavier bulletproof Kevlars. Fillmore had just taken an AK-47 rifle round to the forehead, killing him instantly. The rest of the team behind him was wounded in the same burst of fire. They dove for cover in a narrow alley to the right, dragging Fillmore's lifeless body with them. More Delta assaulters joined them there, while other teams stormed into the adjacent buildings on the right side of the road, seeking cover. Just a short distance ahead of Captain Steele now, I lined up behind a tree on the corner of the alley where the wounded assaulters were being treated. Joined by another Delta assaulter with an M203 grenade launcher, we continued to fire into the berm down the street to our front. From the alley next to us, another assaulter fired around the corner with his SAW light machine gun. At that moment, a small burro started to walk straight toward us, pulling a wagon. We took no chances and cut the animal down.

My training continued to override my senses, and I realized I should be talking to my forward observers and the helicopter gunships, to bring in fire support, rather than engaging in the firefight with the Somalis behind the berm. But the question was, why were none of my forward observers calling? Just minutes prior, around the target building, I had clear communications with the helicopters above and my forward observers on the ground. But now all I was getting in my radio headset was faint static. Moving back from the tree toward Captain Steele and taking scant cover behind a slight rise in the road to my front, I began to go through my checks. I pulled out the handset of my backup radio and was met by a roar of calls from my forward observers. I focused on the calls from Specialist Joe Thomas, who was now in position at the crash site with Lieutenant Tom DiTomasso. I approved his request almost immediately for support from the AH-6 gunships that I knew would now be orbiting overhead and waiting to assist. Thomas radioed back that he had been trying but could not get communication with the gunships on his UHF radio. I told him I would relay his target information and call in the gunships myself. Lying in the middle of the street now I switched over from the smaller radio and got back on the hand mic for the heavy UHF set on my back. Through the increasing roar of combat, smoke, and dust which began to swirl around me, I focused on the call for fire and tried to keep my voice clear and calm, just like we had trained countless times before. I squeezed the rubber block on the hand mic and said, "Barber 51, this is Juliette 36, Fire Mission over." The radio immediately crackled in my ear as the lead attack helicopter pilot Hal Wade responded, "Barber 51, send it." Although I knew he was just a block or two ahead of me, I was unable to observe Thomas' position. I told Thomas to relay the target information for the airstrike. He sent me two separate compass directions along with a distance of 50 meters each, which meant he had more than one threat and they were extremely close, almost at his position. I could understand this, as Rangers just feet away from me were fighting now at close quarters, desperately trying to hold back the closing Somali gunmen. But I also knew I had to give the pilots some room for error. I gave the same compass directions but made the distance 100 meters, still "danger close" but an adequate buffer. Wade acknowledged, and I added that we now had Somalis mixed in with "friendlies."

I yelled over to Captain Steele that I was bringing in an airstrike. Without waiting for approval, I called back over my shoulder to Sean Watson and the other Rangers around us to get "panels out," referring to the orange and red cloth signal panels we carried. These square panels would mark our positions for the pilots orbiting above and allow them to avoid firing into friendlies. As this went on, I remained out in the street, exposed to the enemy fire but lying as low as possible as the rounds cracked over and around me. There was no other choice as I had to keep eyes on the target area so I could observe the Little Bird gun runs and make corrections if needed. I soon heard the approach of the lead Little Bird gunship, being flown by Hal Wade and Randy Jones, as it roared in at rooftop level. I waited tensely for them to engage but, to my surprise, the pilots flew just feet above our position and the fighting on the ground without firing a shot before banking sharply away to the north. The moment the helicopter had appeared overhead, it came under immense fire from the Somalis. The enemy fire sounded like a hailstorm on metal as they poured hundreds of rounds at the Little Bird as it flew by. Wade and Jones had made a dry run to identify our orange panels and the colored smoke grenades we had popped, making deadly sure they knew where we were before they began firing to ensure there would be no fratricide. The gunships always flew in pairs, and the trail Little Bird flown by Tony Kinderer and Larry Kuhlsrude came streaking in next, flying just feet off the rooftops and braving a similar storm of fire. I remembered veterans of Operation *Just Cause* telling stories about the invasion of Panama and of a tragedy involving the gunships. During that past operation when Rangers had called in AH-6 gunships for support, a miscommunication had caused a fratricide event where at least two Rangers from 3rd Battalion were accidentally killed by friendly rocket and minigun fire. Although they were not to blame for the tragic incident in Panama, I knew this weighed heavily on the pilots of the 160th, as they demonstrated now. They were risking everything, even to the point of recklessly exposing themselves and their aircraft to enemy fire, in order to prevent it from happening again.

The firing continued all around me. I lay waiting in the street as new radio calls started to break across the fire support net. The "call for fire" process between a forward observer on the ground and the gunship pilots requires that information be transmitted clearly and understood exactly by both sides. Any mistake or missed information can have deadly results, as had happened in Panama. As the other calls tried to break in across the radio, I ordered them to clear the net and wait.

While I was talking with the gunships, a Delta operator, Sergeant Norm "Hoot" Hooten, appeared in a doorway to my immediate right. He yelled for Captain Steele and me to come in off the street and take cover. As logical as that seemed, at that moment we could not. Rangers were fighting in the streets all around us and as leaders we had to remain there exposed, along with them. Just as importantly for me, I had to be in a position to observe the impact of the gunship rounds and confirm they were on target and striking safely outside of the friendly positions. I could not do that from inside the building.

As seconds passed and I waited for the gunships to come around and line up again, another voice broke in on the radio. It was a faint call saying that "Super 64 was down south of the objective" and needed assistance. Minutes before, when Super 61 had been shot down, our Ranger Blackhawk Super 64 flew back into the target area in accordance with the preestablished contingency plan. Now Super 64 had also been hit by an RPG and crashed about a mile south of us. Still, I was dealing with the threat in front of me. I quickly acknowledged the call, then told them to clear the net as we were at the critical point of calling the fire mission. As I heard the approach of the lead gunship I rose up from my position in the street, trying to see the target area ahead of us even as incoming bullets cracked by my helmet. Just seconds later, I finally heard the AH-6s firing with the chainsaw sound of the Gatling guns, followed by the rip and boom of the 2.75-inch rockets. The firing was so close that spent shell casings rained down on us and we could hear the shriek of the rocket motors before impact. From my position, I raised my head to observe the strikes impacting in the vicinity of the Somalis just past the berm to my north. Reaching back down for the hand mic of the backup radio, I quickly checked in with my forward observer Specialist Joe Thomas to confirm. He responded "fire for effect," telling me the rounds were on target and hitting where we wanted them. I immediately relayed to Wade with the call "continuous suppression, fire for effect," which meant give us all the fire power possible and don't stop shooting. From that point on it seemed that the AH-6 Little Birds fired nonstop, tearing apart the surrounding neighborhoods and breaking the waves of Somali attacks.

Throughout the battle, the gunship pilots stayed overhead above our positions. While I had been calling in the initial fire mission with Wade and Jones in Barber 51, their wingmen in Barber 52 flew behind them. Meanwhile, the other two AH-6 gunships returned to the airfield. In the pilots' seats of these two gunships were Chuck Harrison and Chris Smith in Barber 53 and Jerry Harp and Paul White in Barber 54. Back at the airfield when the helicopters landed, the 160th soldiers on the ground raced around like a NASCAR pit crew to top off the gunships with fuel and ammunition. As soon as the first two gunships ran out of ammunition, the two gunships at the airfield lifted off and came roaring back up over the battle at the crash site to continue the constant aerial attacks. The two lead aircraft then came off station and rotated back to the airfield for their turn to refuel and rearm. The gunship pilots and crews kept up this fighting relay all through the night and into the next day. At the same time that the gunships began their devastating firing runs, the lead elements of our assault group reached the first Blackhawk crash site and went into position with nearly every man fighting to hold the Somalis back.

Even as the Little Birds tore into the Somalis approaching the crash site, there were still numerous gunmen all around us. Just seconds after I sent my last transmission to Barber 51, I felt bullets cracking very close to me and watched them punch two holes into the wall of a metal shed just feet away to my rear. Knowing that Sergeant Keni Thomas and some of the Rangers in his squad were just beyond the shed and behind me, I was afraid they may be firing across my position. I called out "Ranger, Ranger," which was our verbal recognition signal between members of the task force. As I was trying to yell above the growing din, I felt an impact on my right leg like an electric shock followed instantaneously by an explosion of blood and bone. I had been hit by an AK-47 bullet, which shattered my leg and felt like being struck full force by a sledgehammer. The firing came from a Somali gunman who was hidden, unseen behind a stone wall on the other side of the street and just feet away to my left. He had popped up with his AK-47 over the wall and snapped off a ragged burst. As he fired down into our position the third round had struck me in the leg. When the gunman started firing Mike Steele had immediately rolled violently away to his right, then pulled his radio operator with him. His reaction had been automatic to the bullets peppering the streets and walls around us. Both men ran into the immediately adjacent building, which the Delta assaulters had secured just minutes before.

Now I found myself lying wounded and in agony in the dusty street. In shock, I prayed to be able to get home to see Beth and my unborn daughter. I began to drag myself, trying to follow Captain Steele toward the building to my right. Then Delta medic Bart Bullock came charging out of the doorway toward me. As the firefight raged, he grabbed the heavy strap on the back of my armored vest and dragged me out of the firing and through the doorway into a tiny courtyard. Another one of the sergeants pressed me down and tried to reassure me as I struggled to control the pain. Blood poured from my shattered leg, spreading out in a pool around me on the dirty floor of the courtyard. Bullock immediately went to work, reaching into the wreckage of my leg, packing the multiple holes with fistfuls of special clotting bandages. Quickly, he pushed the needle of an IV of fluid into my arm to replace my blood loss. He then half rolled me over, cutting away a flap in my pants to expose my backside, and injected me with a syrette of morphine. The drug rolled in and pushed the intense pain away. He told me to make sure I let any other docs who treated me later know I had already been given one dose of the powerful painkiller. After a few minutes, starting to stabilize, I first asked Bullock if the bleeding had stopped and then for his assessment. He said it was bad, there were a couple of big holes in my leg, but, amazingly, the bleeding had stopped. "Can they save it?" I asked. He was non-committal, but said it may be possible. The initial sight of my blood flowing around me and the damage to my leg left me shocked, but I thanked God for the miracle that the bleeding had stopped. I would deal with the consequences of trying to rehabilitate it later. When Bullock finished working on me, I was eased onto a stretcher and slid farther back into the Somali house. A Somali woman and some small children were huddled there against the wall. In the growing shadows, I could see their wide eyes and wondered how they would remember all of this. One of the Delta assaulters searched the house and found an AK-47, which he immediately disabled.

Outside of the room where the medics worked on my leg, Delta assaulter Norm Hooten was firing out the window and down the street. Just days earlier I had been standing next to Captain Steele in line to get dinner and Hoot was standing in front of us. Steele noticed that the safety switch of the Delta operator's rifle selector was not on "safe" as required in the Ranger Regiment but still on "semi," allowing it to fire. He casually pointed this out to Hoot who then held up his right index finger and said, "This is my safety."

Now, Hoot went into action. Using an M203 40mm grenade launcher, he blew a hole through the wall where the gunman who had shot me was hiding. Charging across the street and through the hole, Norm took the gunman out, then raced back through the Somali fire and into our building. Hoot would eventually earn the Silver Star for his heroism that day.

While we were fighting to hold back the attacks and clear the streets around us, the helicopters above continued to devastate the Somalis. The incredible violence of the AH-6 Little Bird gunships is hard to put into words. After the battle, my forward observers related a story from the aviation support personnel from the 160th who had refueled and rearmed the helicopters all through the 18-hour battle. According to the 160th ground crews, as evening approached during the height of the fighting around the crash site, one of the gunships landed back at the airfield to get gas and ammunition. The pilot asked the ground crew to wipe down his windshield as he could not see through it. As they moved to clean off the front of the aircraft, they were shocked to find the windshield covered in human blood and tissue from the violent air attacks. The pilots related that as the Little Birds hammered the Somali gunmen, bodies were blown into the air, joining the swirling clouds of debris and dust the helicopters passed through on their gun runs.

Fighting around the crash site, the Rangers and operators were standing fast and not yielding. However, the sheer numbers of Somalis fighting against our quickly diminishing force weighed heavily in the balance. The devastating effect of the AH-6 Little Birds allowed us to break the back of the initial Somali assaults and, just as importantly, they worked "in depth," destroying the groups of Somalis who were moving to join the fight. The heroism and skill of these AH-6 gunship pilots, like Hal Wade, Randy Jones, and Chuck Harrison, cannot be emphasized enough. They were absolutely key to our success and survival that night.

While we fought to secure the crash site of Super 61, the aircraft that had carried my fellow Rangers and me in Chalk One into the battle, Blackhawk Super 64, played out its own tragic drama. After inserting our chalk on the southeast corner of the target building earlier in the afternoon, Super 64 had joined the other Blackhawks orbiting safely away from the target area. But when Super 61 went down a few minutes later, it triggered a sequence of actions. First, Super 68 put the Combat Rescue team in by fast-rope onto the wreckage of Super 61. At the same time, Mike Durant and Ray Frank brought Super 64 in to take over Super 61's job flying top cover for the assault force on the ground. As Super 64 approached the target area, another Al Qaeda terrorist with an RPG engaged it, striking the aircraft in the tail section. Both pilots initially assessed there were no serious problems with the aircraft as it continued to fly steady. Then suddenly, the tail rotor assembly disintegrated and the aircraft spun toward the ground, out of control, about a mile south of the first crash site where the battle was raging. All four crewmen – the pilots plus the two door gunners, Tom Fields and Bill Cleveland – were seriously injured but survived the impact.

At this point, the AH-6 Little Birds were focused on supporting our fight around the first crash site. This left Super 62, the other Blackhawk carrying Delta snipers, as the only available aircraft to help. The pilots of Super 62,

Mike Goffena and Jim Yacone, immediately shifted over to the crash site of Super 64 and tried to do what they could to help. They saw the pilots of the downed helicopter, injured but moving in their seats in the cockpit. The aircraft had pancaked, landing relatively flat but hard, which resulted in severe injuries for the crew. Mike Durant struggled in his seat with a broken femur and, next to him, Ray Frank had a badly injured back as well as a broken leg. With the Combat Rescue team and the rest of the assault force committed to the crash of Super 61, there were few options to help the injured crew of Super 64. Super 62 orbited over the crash site and attempted to hold the growing crowds of Somalis back with its door guns and rifle fire from the Delta snipers on board. But as the Somali militiamen began to arrive, the ground fire increased. One of Super 62's crew chiefs manning a door gun was wounded. Delta sniper Brad Halling immediately jumped behind the door gun to take over and continued firing. Super 62 began to take more hits and the pilots knew they would be unable to stay in the air much longer.

The entire task force waited for the reaction force but confidence in their arrival began to ebb. Everyone on board Super 62, as well as those listening on the task force radio net, knew the situation. The promised help was showing no signs of arriving soon and, based on our previous observations of other incidents in the city, its timely arrival would be unlikely. Knowing this, the two remaining Delta snipers on board Super 62, Master Sergeant Gary Gordon and Sergeant First Class Randy Shughart, repeatedly requested that the pilots put them on the ground near the second crash site to assist our wounded comrades of Super 64. Twice these requests were relayed to the officers in the command bird and twice they were denied. Observing the now approaching crowds of Somalis and out of options to save the crew of Super 64, the commanders finally relented, and soon Super 62 landed near the crash. Gordon and Shughart jumped out of the Blackhawk and moved quickly through the alleyways and debris to locate the wreck of Super 64. Moving to the front of the aircraft, they simultaneously engaged approaching Somalis and lifted Mike Durant out of the cockpit. Placing Durant under an overhang, they left him with a rifle and moved back into the fight. Armed only with their sniper rifles, the Delta operators returned to the wreck, taking weapons from the aircraft, and continued to engage the Somali gunmen who approached the crash site.

After dropping off the Delta snipers, Super 62 immediately returned to a close orbit above the wreckage of Super 64 and began to engage the crowds of approaching Somalis. With Somali gunmen now swarming toward the crash site, the ground fire directed at Super 62 intensified.

A Somali gunner with a modified RPG lined the Blackhawk up in his sights. Suddenly, Super 62 was jolted by the impact of a rocket-propelled grenade, which tore off one of the rubber landing gear wheels and wounded one of the pilots as well as Halling, who was sitting behind the door gun. Halling's lower leg had been mangled and the copilot knocked unconscious. The Delta sniper continued to fire while one of his comrades struggled to put a tourniquet in place. The stricken aircraft soon began to shudder and the unwounded pilot, Mike Goffena, was forced to abandon his orbit over the crash site. The Blackhawk limped toward the nearest United Nations base at the New Port area as Goffena struggled to keep it airborne. Barely clearing the perimeter wire, he crash-landed the stricken bird, saving all on board. But this took another task force aircraft out of the fight and left the Americans at the crash site of Super 64 virtually alone.

While the crew aboard Super 62 was attempting to support the men on the ground at the crash site of Super 64, Karl Maier, piloting one of the small MH-6 helicopters, returned from evacuating Dan Busch — the mortally wounded Delta operator — from the original crash site of Super 61. Now intent on doing all he could to help the men at the second crash site, Maier looked for a space to land his small MH-6. Setting his aircraft down a few hundred yards away from the crash site of Super 64, Maier waited for as long as he could for the survivors to emerge.

But with Super 62 knocked out of the fight, the fate of the second crash site was sealed. As the Somalis pressed in, Randy Shughart heard the sound of Gary Gordon cry out as he was hit on the other side of the wreckage. He wished Mike Durant luck and moved back into position with an M16 rifle he had secured from the wreckage of the helicopter. Holding as long as they could, the Americans at the second crash site were finally overwhelmed as the gunmen and mass of the crowd overran the site. As they had done with the Pakistanis and Nigerians earlier in the summer, with brutal and cowardly savagery the Somalis killed the wounded Americans. Amid the wreckage, the Somalis beat and tore at the bodies of the dead American soldiers. The crowd swarmed across the crash site and pushed to the spot where Mike Durant lay injured and nearly helpless off to the side. They immediately attacked the badly wounded pilot with their fists, sticks, and rifle butts. The snarling cloud of Somali faces parted and Durant felt something heavy smash into his face. Looking up from the ground, he saw that one Somali had begun to beat him with the severed arm of one of the dead Americans. Suddenly gunshots rang out, warning the attackers away. There was momentary hesitation and some argument before the crowd closed back in and seized Durant, lifting him above their heads, out of the wreckage and into the nearby streets. Years later it was learned that a rival militia group had come to the crash site and intervened to spare Durant in order to ransom him back to the Habr Gidr and Somali National Alliance. Later, after the ransom was paid the wounded pilot was taken to Aideed's forces and secured by the SNA for the purposes of negotiation with the U.S. None of this was known to the task force at the time. For days Durant's status was unknown until the SNA finally released a shadowy videotape of the injured pilot being interviewed in his prison room. The week the video came out pictures from it appeared on the cover of every major news magazine in the United States. The full story of his capture would emerge over the following years, pieced together through debriefings and journalists' interviews with the Somalis.

While the drama played out at the second crash site with Super 64, the Ranger convoy continued on its own tragic odyssey. Following its arrival at the target building, the convoy had been positioned just a short distance from the crash site only blocks away. After Super 61 had gone down the assault force was able to quickly move on foot to the crash site, but the convoy could not follow the same route through the narrow warren of streets. Having to move with both the HMMVs and the much larger 5-ton trucks, the convoy was forced to split away and travel along the broad thoroughfares. They intended to drive just a few blocks and then turn into an intersection adjacent to the crash site. This was a forlorn hope.

The convoy had been in contact with the enemy since its arrival near the target building earlier in the mission. When they had first arrived, as the vehicles waited to be called forward to the target building, the Somalis had begun to fire on them. A rocket-propelled grenade struck one of the three large 5-ton trucks and disabled it. The driver and his partner were able to escape the vehicle and load onto another truck. Soon after the convoy was called forward to the target building, Jeff Struecker had been sent on his mission to evacuate Blackburn. The overall mission had then changed with the downing of Super 61. The convoy was now ordered to move to the crash site of Super 61, bringing along the Somali prisoners and some of the assault force who were already loaded up and onboard the trucks. But events began to conspire against the task force at this point and the convoy suffered the brunt of the consequences.

The Somalis were experienced street fighters in the heart of their home ground. They barricaded the narrow avenues approaching the crash site with burning tires and the wrecks of cars. The clock was also working against us as we had now been on the ground for over an hour, and the Somalis were massing in the thousands and approaching the contact area, guided by the usual system of burning tires. As the trucks departed the initial target building, moving along the main thoroughfares, they were met with a storm of small-arms and RPG fire. The convoy passed through this gauntlet of fire, exposed in their unarmored vehicles, and halted, unable to turn down the narrow and barricaded road to the crash site. Trying to navigate with only general references through the streets and under intense fire, the convoy commander, Lieutenant Colonel McKnight, pleaded for assistance from the aircraft overhead to find a viable route. As instructions were sent down from the various aircraft, including the P-3 Orion surveillance plane, they had to pass through multiple layers of communications from the command bird before finally reaching McKnight. Anyone who has led a convoy knows this is a difficult proposition under the best of conditions. In a maelstrom of enemy fire and the chaos of combat, it is all but impossible. The Rangers assigned to the vehicles, along with those who had jumped on board with the Somali prisoners, fought back desperately against the fire coming from all sides. The convoy's heavy weapons, the .50-caliber machine guns and MK19 grenade launchers mounted on the trucks, roared continually as other Americans fired their weapons out of the windows and over the sides of the vehicles. But the concentrated fire of the Somalis began to take its toll. Some of the vehicles were hit and disabled by rocket-propelled grenades, forcing the Americans to bail out. Under heavy fire, Delta operators and Rangers began to fall in the street and onboard the vehicles.

Amid the growing chaos, Sergeant Casey Joyce took a position on a street corner and fired back at the Somalis as the convoy attempted to turn. Joyce, who had anxiously followed me in the telephone line just the day before, suddenly took an AK-47 round through his back where the protective vest had no armored plate. The round went through his body, struck the front plate, and bounced back into him, fatally wounding him. Seeing Joyce fall, other Rangers quickly moved to secure their wounded comrade. His buddies loaded Joyce into the back of a truck, while Corporal James Cavaco provided covering fire with a MK19 in one of the truck turrets. Suddenly, Cavaco was also struck by a round and died as he slid down inside of the vehicle.

One of the luckiest Rangers in the convoy that day was Specialist Adalberto "Rod" Rodriguez. Dismounted from his vehicle and fighting in the street, Rod was hit by multiple bursts of AK-47 fire that stitched him across his back and down his leg, as well as across his chest and head. Thankfully, despite taking multiple wounds, his protective vest and Kevlar helmet stopped five of the AK-47 rounds. The Rangers of his platoon picked him up off the street and threw him in the back of a HMMV, which also held Delta operator Master Sergeant Tim "Griz" Martin. Martin was well known in the task force in part due to his badly scarred face resulting from a previous accident, but also because he was one of the most amiable and competent Delta operators in the assault force. He had climbed on board the truck back at the target building to help secure the Somali prisoners. Aboard that same HMMV another one of my forward observers, Private First Class Chris Carlson, provided covering fire as the injured Rodriguez was loaded on the truck. Carlson felt an explosion rock the truck, deafening him as another RPG struck and blew Griz Martin and Rod out the back of the vehicle. The rocket wounded Rod again, tearing off the back of his left thigh, but Griz took the brunt of the blast in the lower half of his torso. Fatally wounded, he was somehow managing to still cling to life.

Driving the 5-ton truck immediately behind Martin and Rodriguez' HMMV, Ranger John Maddox had been under AK-47 fire since the moment they had arrived at the target building. Soon, both Maddox and the other Ranger in the vehicle's cab, Sergeant Spaulding, were wounded and the vehicle badly damaged but they continued on. Maddox struggled to control the big truck when it took more hits, and the brakes began to fail. When the HMMV in front of him took the blast of the RPG round and crashed to a halt, it threw the wounded Rodriguez into the street. Unable to stop his truck, Maddox barreled over Rodriguez, dragging him under the bumper as he crashed into the wreck of the HMMV in front of him. Somehow, Rodriguez survived this too. Finding him alive, Rangers quickly pulled him out of the vehicle wreckage and threw him in the back of Maddox's truck along with the dying Griz Martin.

The convoy's situation was not improving. It had now cleared the main gauntlet of fire but missed the turn again. The aircraft orbiting overhead, far above the chaotic maelstrom of the battle, directed it to turn around and go back the way it had come. Things now began to all but disintegrate for the convoy. More vehicles were hit and disabled and there were more casualties every minute. When a Ranger manning a .50-cal. machine gun in the turret of one of the HMMV trucks went down with a wound, he was immediately replaced by Ranger Sergeant Lorenzo Ruiz. Minutes later, Ruiz took an AK-47 round in the stomach, just under his bulletproof plate. Tough but amiable, Ruiz bravely insisted he was alright but died later, alongside Griz Martin in the casualty collection point at the airfield.

One of the two remaining 5-ton trucks in the convoy was being driven by Private First Class Richard Kowalewski. Along with the rest of the convoy, Kowalewski's truck was being raked by Somali fire until he was finally wounded in the shoulder by an AK-47 round. As his buddy Clay Othic, seated next to him in the cab, tried to apply a pressure dressing, Kowalewski, or "Alphabet" as he was called by his fellow Rangers, said he was okay and kept driving. Kowalewski exulted to his friend that he would now get a Purple Heart for being wounded in action. Seconds later, the vehicle rocked with the impact of a rocket-propelled grenade that slammed through the driver-side door. The round hit Kowalewski squarely in the side, severing his left arm and killing him instantly. The rocket had penetrated the steel door but failed to detonate, remaining impaled in the young Ranger's chest, tail fins and nose protruding out either side of his body. Othic pulled the dead Ranger out of the cab as they abandoned the vehicle and loaded him into the back of Maddox's badly damaged truck, the last remaining 5-ton. Later, after arriving back at the airfield, medical crews were shocked to find the live rocket still protruding from Kowalewski's chest. The medical staff quietly moved the young Ranger's body out of the casualty collection point and further away down the tarmac to be diffused by the military bomb experts from the explosive ordnance disposal team.

After Kowalewski's truck was destroyed and the convoy had managed to turn around through the maze of city streets, it was raked yet again in the gauntlet of Somali fire. The convoy's situation now became a question of survival. Down to one barely running 5-ton and a few shot-up HMMVs, almost everyone – including the Somali prisoners – had been hit.

The platoon sergeant for the Rangers and second in command on the convoy was Sergeant First Class Bob Gallagher. I knew him well as he had previously been in Alpha Company with me before he moved over to take a platoon in neighboring Bravo Company earlier that year. He was known by everyone as a great leader who was always cool and upbeat. As Lieutenant Colonel McKnight tried to lead the convoy, Gallagher rode in his assigned position at the rear of the convoy. As things began to come apart, he moved forward, running up and down the convoy, helping the wounded, directing the fight, and trying to find out why the convoy seemed adrift. Gallagher was struck twice while the convoy was running the gauntlet of fire, wounded once in the arm and then again in the opposite shoulder. Unable to use the hand of his wounded arm to work his radio hand mic properly, he held it against his ear with his good shoulder and keyed it with the opposite unwounded hand. As the convoy tried to turn around, Gallagher ran to the front, through the intense gunfire, and found Lieutenant Colonel McKnight in the lead vehicle. The bulletproof windshield on McKnight's vehicle had been shattered by gunfire and the commander was slightly wounded. Considering the carnage in men and vehicles behind them in the rest of the convoy, the decision was made to call off the attempt to reach the crash site and turn back. Gallagher took the lead now and the convoy pushed south toward the airfield, still fighting but crawling along with just a few vehicles left running, including one truck pushing another that had been disabled. Every vehicle was loaded with casualties. With the wounded thrown on top of the dead, the crippled convoy reached the main traffic circle north of the airfield. The Rangers and operators on the convoy continued to fight but the situation was desperate.

Back at the airfield, the tactical operations center personnel watched the raid and then the widening battle unfold on the video screens. Everyone there knew how desperate the situation was. Gathering a few remaining vehicles from a recently returned convoy of Rangers who had been away on a logistics run that morning, Major Craig Nixon, my former company commander and one of the Ranger staff officers, strove to put together a second Ranger convoy to join the fight. The immediate intent for this second convoy was to try to rescue the Americans at the second crash site of Super 64 where Gordon and Shughart were just getting on the ground. To form this convoy Nixon was able to scrape together a handful of HMMV trucks, only a few of which were lightly armored, and even those could not stop rifle or automatic weapons fire.

When the task force had initially been formed back at Fort Bragg, the military planners had seen the need for armored vehicles to move through the streets we knew would be controlled by Somali gunmen. But the Clinton Administration had rejected the request for armored vehicles. The task force had only been allowed to deploy to Somalia with the minimum force necessary to conduct the search and raids to capture Aideed. This direct guidance from the highest levels had also forced the leadership of the task force to cut the additional platoon of Rangers from Alpha Company, which had originally been assembled for the mission at Fort Bragg. Along with the additional manpower and armored vehicles, our request for Air Force AC-130 gunships was also disapproved. As the battle became more desperate these thoughts now circled like dark ravens.

Nixon quickly put together the convoy with what the task force had left for manpower. Joining the vehicles and crews from the infantry platoon, cooks, supply sergeants, and clerks now volunteered to join the new convoy. These Rangers illustrated the ethos of the 75th Ranger Regiment. While it is the job of the infantry line platoons to conduct combat operations, every Ranger, no matter what his specialty or specific job, must be prepared to fight and display the warrior spirit. The extreme circumstances and maelstrom of battle on this day in Mogadishu would now require them to live up to the Ranger Creed.

Among the Ranger leaders joining the convoy was my friend Lieutenant Scott Spellmeyer, new to B Company like I was. Spellmeyer was in charge of the mortars and other support weapons for the company. With no role on our raid missions for these heavy weapons, Spellmeyer was essentially out of a job. He immediately stepped up to join the second convoy now being formed. Also climbing aboard the trucks of this second convoy was another Ranger I knew well, Specialist Dale Sizemore. Sizemore had broken an arm earlier in the week playing volleyball. As the second convoy assembled, he sawed the cast off his arm before gingerly putting on his combat gear and mounting up.

Another one of the leaders who joined the second convoy was Sergeant First Class Rick Lamb who was then serving on the small staff in the tactical operations center. Rick Lamb was another Army legend – a lantern-jawed combat veteran and poster child for the Ranger Regiment with years of experience serving in its ranks. He was a veteran of numerous Ranger combat operations to include *Desert One* and the Iranian hostage rescue mission. Lamb and Spellmeyer each took charge of vehicles and teams of Rangers.

Major Nixon, the senior officer, very quickly briefed the convoy and immediately they set out. The immediate intent for this second convoy was to try to rescue the Americans at the crash site of Super 64 where Gordon and Shughart were just getting on the ground. The planned route for the second convoy was to travel northwest in the direction of the target area where the battle now raged until they hit the major landmark of the K4 Traffic Circle. At that point they intended to turn east in order to locate the second crash site. Almost immediately upon leaving the airfield, AK-47 rifle fire began to crack over and around the convoy as it travelled along the main roads. This did not significantly slow the convoy as Nixon guided it north, and soon the traffic circle could be seen in the distance. As the second convoy approached the traffic circle, smoking military vehicles could be seen approaching from the north. Nixon brought the convoy abruptly to a halt and directed them to temporary positions. The turret gunners kept up covering fire as what was left of the first Ranger convoy, now led by Gallagher after McKnight had been wounded, began arriving at the traffic circle. The sight of the first convoy was shocking, with vehicles piled high, carrying heaps of wounded on top of the dead, and every vehicle badly damaged.

As the two groups of Rangers began to link up, it was obvious the situation was critical for the survivors of the first convoy and they needed assistance to make it back to the airfield. Nixon, McKnight, and Gallagher briefly gathered around the vehicles in the middle of the street near the traffic circle. The decision was made to help the first convoy get its survivors back to the airfield, and reorganize. there for another try to reach the crash site of Super 64. Every turret gunner and able-bodied man blazed away out the truck windows and over the sides, hammering a path through the streets. An eternity later the combined convoy finally arrived back at the airfield.

As it pulled up to the main gate, Gallagher, still in the lead vehicle, jumped out of his vehicle and painfully ran forward. The Egyptian soldiers of the United Nations force guarding the gate hesitated to move, in shock by the sight of the blood-soaked warrior and the smoking carnage of vehicles behind him. Without time to explain the situation, he forcefully ordered the gate to be opened and soon the convoy was through. With multiple wounds and covered in his own blood and that of his men, Gallagher, through his fearless leadership, had gotten the convoys back to the airfield. It would not be the last time his leadership would be decisive while wounded on the battlefield. Later promoted to command sergeant major, Bob Gallagher would add to his legend in the coming decades during numerous battles and deployments in Iraq.

Once back inside the compound the Rangers of the second convoy and base medical personnel swarmed around the damaged vehicles, carrying off the wounded and unloading the dead. The scenes inside the bullet-riddled, blood-covered vehicles were hellacious, stunning many of the Rangers and operators. While the casualties were quickly unloaded, the Somali prisoners who remained unhurt were put in the holding pen. After doing what they could for their wounded comrades the second convoy began to re-form. They were joined by the surviving Rangers and operators of the first convoy.

Nixon now led this reinforced convoy out again, trying to reach the crash site of Super 64 and the beleaguered Americans there. He was joined in his command vehicle by one of my forward observers, Sergeant Raleigh Cash. Using the more powerful vehicle radios as well as relaying through some of the orbiting helicopters, Cash and the convoy were able to sporadically communicate with us back at the first crash site. Although the reports were sketchy, it kept our hope momentarily alive as we knew the task force was still trying to reach the crash site of Super 64 and then hopefully join us at the first crash site.

But as the convoy rolled out the gate it was immediately engaged by heavy fire from the Somalis. Primed and ready, the Rangers and operators on the convoy responded immediately with machine-gun and rifle fire, cutting down the Somalis shooting from the street and windows around them as they roared north. As the firing increased, the convoy discovered the city was now alive with fire and the Somalis had not been idle. Barricades of burning tires and wrecked cars blocked the main routes. Like the first convoy, they found themselves making awkward turns down side streets looking for alternate ways forward. As more vehicles were hit and casualties increased, the ring of Somalis and burning barricades seemed to close in on the convoy. It soon became obvious they would be unable to penetrate to the second crash site. Nixon consulted with the tactical operations center and was informed that a larger, additional force was trying to assemble. With little to no hope of success on their current attempt, he ordered the convoy back to the airfield. As we continued to hold out at the first crash site, we soon realized that for the time being we were alone.

Upon arrival back at the airfield, what was left of the two convoys from the task force received word that the 10th Mountain Division quick reaction force and other United Nations forces were now preparing to assist. This force was assembling at the New Port facility not far from the airfield. The Rangers and Delta operators who had survived the first two convoys now began integrating into the larger United Nations effort. The United Nations force being hastily assembled included the 10th Mountain Division soldiers, as well as Pakistani tanks and Malaysian armored troop carriers. When the men of Task Force Ranger arrived at the New Port they found vehicles in various stages of lining up and soldiers waiting for instructions. The Rangers and operators knew the assault force was still out at the crash site desperately fighting and holding on. Worse, there was no word on the fate of the Americans at the second crash site. Finally, late in the night, the various American units were combined with the Pakistani tanks and Malaysian armored cars and the convoy set off north into the city.

Finally, after what seemed like an eternity, the United Nations convoy began to ponderously move forward. Initially, the convoy moved through areas of Mogadishu which were not controlled by Aideed's Habr Gidr clan. Some of the people of these neighborhoods, hearing the sounds of battle in the distance, came out to cheer the United Nations on against their rivals. Still leading a team of Rangers in the convoy, Rick Lamb had to restrain his jittery soldiers from firing at these friendly Somalis. Soon, however, the convoy began to encounter Aideed's forces and the battle was on again. As the Somali fire increased, the vehicles in the convoy began to take hits, causing more casualties, especially among the Rangers in their unarmored vehicles. Rick Lamb's HMMV driver was suddenly hit by an AK-47 round that badly wounded his hand. Taking over for the wounded driver, Lamb pushed his heavy Kevlar helmet back slightly and wiped his face. Just at that moment a Somali fired a rocket-propelled grenade at his vehicle from down a street to his right. Lamb tracked the rocket as it hit and skimmed off the hood of his truck then impacted the wall immediately to his left. Shrapnel and concrete peppered Lamb through the open side of the truck as the explosion rang in his ears. The explosion caused Lamb to black out momentarily. But he came to with a sharp pain in his forehead, then reached up to find blood running down his face. Still under fire, Lamb kept control of the vehicle and pushed on with the convoy.

Back at the first crash site with the assault force, more wounded were brought into the casualty collection point and laid all around me. The Rangers and Delta operators continued to furiously and methodically clear the streets and courtyards immediately around us. The devastating fire of the Little Birds continued to chew into the neighborhoods as we fortified the short stretch of buildings we occupied, and consolidated into a tight perimeter.

The crash site of Super 61 was a block away and out of sight from where I lay in the Somali house with many other wounded Rangers and Delta operators. Mike Steele was nearby talking on the radio to Lieutenant Colonel Harrell in the command bird and to the commander of the Delta operators nearby at the crash site while trying, at the same time, to direct his Rangers and account for casualties. Early in the fight, Steele had received a radio call from Sergeant Jeff Struecker who, at that time, was still driving toward the airfield to evacuate the injured Private Blackburn. Struecker reported that he had taken additional casualties. When Captain Steele asked for a status on their condition, there was a pause. Captain Steele repeated the request and, after another moment of hesitation, Struecker replied, "red," meaning killed in action (KIA). For a moment, time stopped for everyone who was listening. We all knew the fighting was intense and that we were taking casualties, but this confirmation of the first KIA was a soul-shaking blow of reality. Then the roar of combat brought us back to the present.

Daylight began to fade but the fight continued. Coming in from the fire-swept street, Sergeant Randy Ramaglia burst into the room where the wounded were laid out on the blood-soaked dirt floor. He gathered weapons and ammunition, shifting Rangers into better firing positions and exhorting others before charging back into the firefight.

As night came, things began to gradually stabilize in our stretch of street. For the present, the immediate area had been cleared and the Somali gunmen neutralized. With the Little Birds constantly prowling and firing above us, the firefight on the ground lulled back into random contact and occasional incoming.

The decision not to bring night vision goggles was now proving costly. There were a few sets available, mainly taken from the wreck of the helicopter. Still, the night gave us other advantages. We put out strobe lights and used lasers, actually making it easier for the orbiting aircraft to identify our positions than in the daytime. While the Somalis were having great difficulty seeing or accurately engaging in the dark, that advantage did not completely secure us or protect the helicopters. Hours into the siege, when a Blackhawk approached our position after dark to try to provide some resupply, it was met with withering fire from the surrounding Somalis. The helicopter received multiple hits and was nearly brought down on top of us as its crew hastily pushed out the bags of desperately needed ammunition and medical supplies. While the pilots were able to successfully land back at the airfield, this ended the ongoing debate among our leaders about bringing in an aircraft to evacuate the wounded.

While unavoidable, this decision proved tragically fatal for Corporal Jamie Smith, who had sat to my right on Super 64 and been alongside me again in the perimeter earlier in the day. After we had moved away from the target building, as the combined group moved to the crash site, Smith had pushed ahead with other members of his squad. During the furious fighting around the crash site, an AK-47 round tore through his pelvis and severed his femoral artery. Smith had fought to hang on for hours, but despite the medics' struggle to keep him alive, in the dark hours of the night he finally gave his life.

From the time we established the perimeter and continuing through the night, the question was repeatedly asked about reinforcements: "When will the QRF get here?" We were in the middle of Habr Gidr territory, filled with hundreds of thousands of Somalis. We had seen from the air, and observed down the alleys and streets, the massive crowds and swarming militia. Our numbers had been reduced from the start with the departure of the vehicle convoy, taking not only the Somali prisoners but part of our assault force. Even with the addition of the Combat Rescue team, we were fewer than 100 soldiers at the crash site. Now, after hours of fierce fighting, most of our force had been killed or wounded.

Through the night, I lay in the casualty collection point, my leg a dull throb through a morphine haze as I listened to Captain Steele on the radio. Our position was an island in the sea of Somali attacks. We knew that our comrades continuing the fight around us would never give up or let anything penetrate our tiny perimeter. We also had the Little Birds overhead with the comforting rip of Gatling guns and boom of their rockets. But we needed help – more

Americans to get in the fight and help get our wounded and dead out and back to the airfield.

I once met an old veteran from the 101st Airborne Division who had been surrounded by the Germans at Bastogne during the Battle of the Bulge in World War II. Someone asked him if he was grateful to Patton for rescuing them. I will always remember the hard look on his face when he replied, "We didn't need rescue, we just needed someone else to come out there and get in the fight with us!" That is exactly how we felt that night as we waited through the long hours.

Over the coming hours, as the assault force hung on to the perimeter around the first crash site, we slowly received reports of these efforts and continued to wait. Finally, we heard the thunderous approach of the relief convoy. We could mark its progress as it drew closer by the amount of firing we could hear. The noise grew in intensity to a crescendo as it crept forward from intersection to intersection.

The convoy was laying down a tremendous amount of firepower as it moved slowly and methodically through the Somali neighborhoods. Our anxiety rose as the last thing we wanted was to get blown away by the .50-calibers and MK19s of the 10th Mountain troops and the mixed force of the UN convoy. Deliberate instructions and warnings were passed to the convoy before one brave Ranger ran out from the crash site to mark our position with additional chemlites as a recognition signal. We waited tensely until the radio call came back that the convoy had identified the chemlites. A few more minutes passed until we heard vehicles racing up the alley. American HMMVs arrived first and moved through our positions and past us to the wreckage of Super 61. Next came heavily armored cars from the Malaysian Army. We were anxious to begin moving, but officers from the 10th Mountain Division arrived and insisted on getting one of their doctors into the casualty collection point first. Our eagerness to get loaded was misplaced as there was still work to do on the wreck to extract Wolcott's body.

Super 61 had come down flat on its belly but struck a wall on impact and pitched violently forward onto its nose, crushing the two pilots. Donovan Briley's side of the aircraft had remained relatively upright and his body had been freed without much difficulty. But Wolcott was essentially underneath the wreck and pinned tightly with the weight of the aircraft on top of him. In order to get his body out, the soldiers and vehicles of the quick reaction force were put to work trying to pull the wreckage apart, but with limited success.

Meanwhile, the soft glow of morning slowly began to creep into the dark and we knew the fight would be on again in earnest. As the wounded waited on stretchers to be loaded in the vehicles, chains were finally used to pull Wolcott's body from the wreckage of the aircraft. Minutes continued to pass and we were finally loaded in the back of the Malaysian vehicles. While these vehicles had armor against rifle fire and light machine guns, I knew a rocket-propelled grenade could penetrate them and incinerate everyone inside. As I was still strapped into my stretcher and unable to move, this was the tensest time for me during the battle and we urged the driver to get going. The Malaysians looked anxious as they offered cigarettes and shared bottles of water with us. Finally, as the morning broke and the sky began to get lighter, everyone who could be was loaded and the convoy lurched forward. Somali fire increased, and the Malaysian gunner above me in the turret squeezed off bursts from his machine gun, raining me with hot shell casings. Riding inside those vehicles, what we did not know was that there had not been enough room on the HMMVs and armored cars for all of the task force. The unwounded Rangers and Delta operators were forced to trail the convoy on foot, running through the streets and across intersections. This final push to safety has become known as the "Mogadishu Mile" and is often commemorated today with road races and endurance events.

After a tense, halting drive out of the Habr Gidr neighborhoods with the Somali fire increasing, things suddenly began to grow quieter outside. The Malaysian vehicles made a last turn and surged through the gates of a soccer stadium before coming to an abrupt halt. We were inside the stadium housing the Pakistani Army contingent and I knew that a portion of our ordeal was over.

8

Borne the Battle

In war one learns thoroughly but the tuition is high.
Ernst Jünger, Storm of Steel

As the convoy roared through the stadium gates housing the Pakistani Army contingent and pulled up along the sidelines of the soccer field, Americans from the task force and medical personnel crowded around the vehicles. Within seconds of my armored car coming to a halt, the rear doors opened onto a sea of American faces. As the morning sunlight shone into the cramped space inside the vehicle, I looked up at my comrades with relief as my stretcher was lifted out of the back. One of the first to greet me was Rick Lamb who was also injured but was up and walking around. With a bandage wrapped around his head, he looked like the wounded drummer in the famous painting of the patriots of the Revolution. He grabbed one side of my stretcher as I was carried to the sideline of the soccer field. Typically stoic and almost nonchalant about his wound, Lamb let the other "more serious" cases get loaded onto the medevac helicopters first before finally climbing aboard later in the morning. After getting some cursory treatment and cleaning the blood off his face, he soon left the hospital and hitched a ride back to the task force compound. Days later, migraine headaches caused doctors to take an X-ray of Sergeant Lamb's head. They were shocked to find a piece of shrapnel from the rocket lodged deep inside the front of his brain, precisely between the lobes. Masterful Army neurosurgeons cut into his head and took off the front of his skull to delicately conduct surgery on his brain. While they were able to stabilize and repair the damage, the shrapnel itself was too deep to remove and was left in place. With his typical determination, Lamb would return to duty just a few weeks after the surgery.

As Lamb and the other Rangers set my stretcher down amid the sea of wounded, one of my FOs, Sergeant Raleigh Cash, spotted me and hurried over. Cash was another one of the stalwart veteran FO sergeants in B Company and had been assigned to the Ranger convoy. Along with Major Nixon, he took part in the relief attempts of the previous day. He later came back out with the Rangers in the larger UN relief effort that fought its way to the crash site early that morning. As I spoke to Sergeant Cash, he was joined by Specialist Joe Thomas who had been on the crash site. Along with Butch Galliete, these three Rangers were the only ones from my nine-man fire support team who were miraculously unscathed in the fighting. Looking past them as we spoke, I could see that up and down the sideline of

the field were rows of stretchers with wounded Rangers and
Delta operators. At the far end of the field by the goal post,
I could also see a shorter line of shapes wrapped in ponchos
and realized the cost had been higher than I knew. As my
comrades gave me bits and pieces of information, I asked
about my aircraft, Super 64, and was told, "we don't know."

Almost immediately, medics approached me and began to
check my wound. I was still worried about the bleeding and
knew I had lost a lot of blood. As the medevac helicopters
began to cycle in to land on the soccer field, I told the
medics I had been hit the day before around 1700 hours.
Remembering what Bart Bullock had told me, I repeated a
number of times that I had already had one shot of morphine
and had been hit 14 hours ago. It soon began to register
with the medics the length of time that I had literally been
living on the IV bags. They quickly reacted and brought
my stretcher out to the landing zone as a "priority," loading
me aboard the next U.S. helicopter. Lifting steeply out of
the stadium to avoid ground fire, it was a short flight across
the city to the old American embassy compound, where
more medical teams were waiting on the helicopter pad.
As we set down at the 46th Combat Support Hospital, the
medics surged up to the side door of the medevac aircraft.
They untangled my IV lines from the rigging of the
helicopter and slid my stretcher onto a gurney, wheeling
me with controlled urgency straight to pre-op. This was
my first introduction to the incredible network of dedicated
professionals who make up the U.S. Army medical system.

Although the soldiers at the landing pad had been U.S. medics, I was soon surprised to see a tall, blonde military doctor from the German Bundeswehr approach my table as they prepped me for surgery. As the anesthetic began to hit, I gave him a "Wie geht's?" and, remembering Herr Gundel from The Citadel, figured I was in good hands. I told him my name was Lechner and that I was German, too. He smiled reassuringly and, just before the anesthetic began to put me under, explained in good English that they were going to do a "debridement," a cleaning and disinfecting of the wound. It would be alright. "Alles gut," he told me as I faded out.

I awoke hours later being wheeled into a long green Army tent and immediately recognized everyone in the beds around me. The tent was full of wounded Rangers and Delta operators, most of them heavily bandaged, with every kind of wound. We had been cleaned up to some extent and our uniforms cut away, replaced with blue hospital gowns. We didn't talk much, still trying to adjust to the circumstances and our surroundings. It was late morning now and a nurse brought me some scrambled eggs and toast. It was the first meal I had eaten since having an MRE early the day before in what seemed like another lifetime. As the nurses in our tent talked, they seemed stunned at the number of wounded coming in and angry at the Somalis. They made a point of telling us the hospital was now turning away any Somali who came to be treated. That night, we heard incoming fire in the distance and the machine guns on the nearby guard posts opening up along the perimeter. With no weapons and wearing only a hospital gown, I began to feel vulnerable again. The next morning, things got better when more visitors from TF Ranger came over from the airfield. It was reassuring to see our comrades from TF Ranger, still confident and ready to take the fight back out to the enemy, especially where our missing comrades were concerned. The Rangers and Delta operators in the hospital who were lightly wounded were similarly anxious to get back to the unit and into the line. However, we had been profoundly changed and were still absorbing the shock of battle.

On missions prior to the raid on October 3, we had made scattered contact with the enemy and even taken some wounded, but we were not convinced that made us "combat veterans." Those encounters just didn't seem to meet the threshold of our expectations passed on to us from World War II, Korea, and Vietnam veterans. But after the battle on October 3 and 4, the issue was beyond doubt, as if we had passed over a chasm and there was no going back. There was a saying in the American Civil War that, when you had been in combat, you had "seen the elephant." In those days, this probably referred to the "big show" or circus, but it was also fitting for me because what we had been through in those 18 odd hours was unquestionably the full scale of combat experience. Not only had I been wounded, like most of my comrades, but I had killed the enemy. I had fired my weapon at Somali gunmen, but I never knew if I hit any of them. Regardless, as the fire support officer, I had called for and directed the AH-6 gunships that had devastated those first waves of Somalis, killing scores of them right off the bat. As a Christian, I had anticipated feeling guilty about these potential circumstances, if it ever came to pass that I would orchestrate and bring about the death of my enemies. To my surprise, I felt no guilt but only grim satisfaction. For that, I felt guilty.

Talking to other wounded or soldiers from the task force who came over from the airfield, we began to piece together stories from the fight. We were amazed at the myriad separate events and chaos that had occurred over the previous 24 hours. The scope of the battle went far beyond the fighting at the target building and first crash site that I had personally experienced. Listening to the other Rangers, we gradually began to grasp the intensity of the convoy battles. There was still no word on Super 64's crew or the two Delta snipers who had gone in to help them. We learned of the casualties on the Ranger convoy and more of our friends who hadn't made it.

Later that morning, as I lay on my cot with my leg wrapped in bandages, doctors began to make their rounds. As one group unwrapped the bandages to examine my leg, I could see the shock on their faces. One of them asked another, "What did that, an RPG?" None of that was encouraging and, as the wrappings came off, I only stole brief looks down at the cavernous wounds and my mangled leg.

The AK-47 round had struck me a couple of inches below my right knee. Coming from above and behind me, it had blown a huge hole in the front of my lower leg, leaving a 4-inch gap in the upper portion of my tibia, eviscerating my leg as it traveled downward, ripping another 6-inch hole along the inside of my calf, and exiting just above my ankle. As the bone had exploded, its jagged pieces became shards of shrapnel and punched numerous other smaller holes in my leg. The initial debridement procedure had stopped the bleeding while also cleaning up my leg, but there was little the doctors and staff at the 46th could do beyond that. Combat Support Hospitals (CSHs) were the descendants of the famous Mobile Army Surgical Hospital (MASH) units and were designed to save the critically wounded, patching them up and stabilizing them for transport to the rear.

During the battle on October 3 and 4, and in the days that followed, the doctors and medical staff of the 46th CSH would carry on the great traditions of Army surgeons and combat medicine. A hospital with just 52 beds and a handful of doctors and nurses, they took in 90 casualties and performed 34 major surgeries in a single day, with the treatment continuing on through the week until the wounded were evacuated home. Unlike more conventional conflicts such as *Desert Storm*, where there was a front line, the 46th was based in a compound in the heart of Mogadishu with SNA militia prowling just outside the wire, launching mortars and taking pot shots. The men and women of the 46th CSH were the first in a long line of incredible and dedicated medical personnel I would meet in the coming months.

While I was being treated at the 46th CSH, my wounds had been stabilized, but any chance of saving my leg would require extensive surgery. The doctors soon told me I would be going out on the next medevac flight. I was scheduled to board a U.S. Air Force C-141 transport, along with the rest of the wounded headed to Landstuhl, Germany. After another night in the university compound with the 46th CSH, we were finally wheeled out to the landing pad and lifted out by helicopter to fly back to the TF Ranger compound at the airfield. Landing not far from the hangar and TOC, we were met by our TF Ranger comrades. They carried our stretchers off the helicopters and lined us up in rows outside the small U.S. Air Force medical facility where we waited to load the big green C-141 transport.

While I lay there on the airfield tarmac, many of my comrades came by to link up and offer encouragement. Norm Hooten knelt down and told me the story of what he had seen on the street and how he had taken out the Somali gunman who shot me. Other Rangers came by as well; then, Colonel Boykin knelt down and asked how I was doing. When he asked about my leg, I told him the doctors "didn't know." Before the Air Force medics pushed in to do my pre-flight check, Colonel Boykin knelt down and prayed for the Lord to watch over me. Minutes later, our comrades carried us onto the C-141 and locked our stretchers onto the vertical stack of racks for the flight to Germany.

On the rack below me, a soldier from the 10th Mountain was strapped in, still wrapped in bandages and breathing on a respirator. He did not look good and would later die at the hospital in Landstuhl.

Once locked in aboard the C-141, I was in the competent hands of the Air Force medical personnel but began to feel cut off from my TF Ranger comrades. While the danger had passed, I felt like my armor had been taken away. The only thing that had stood between us and the Somali crowds was the handful of Americans holding those street corners by flying low above the rooftops. I felt alone, as if I had been separated from my "patrol" or team and continued to feel that way as we landed in Germany. At the U.S. Air Force hospital in Landstuhl, I was eventually put into the first real bed I had seen in over two months.

Days later, reality slowly intruded on the shock that was still wearing off. On a small TV in my room, I watched the coup attempt in Moscow against Boris Yeltsin. The anchor quickly wrapped up the news from Russia to show a shadowy video from a house in Mogadishu, and there on the screen was Mike Durant, beaten and dirty, but alive. His Somali captors and a news crew spoke to him while he looked to be in shock. It was just days since my last conversation with Mike in the hangar as we had moved toward our aircraft, but it seemed like a lifetime. I was elated, along with the rest of the wounded Rangers in the hospital, to see Mike in that video and hoped to find more survivors, but we knew the crash site had been overrun. More news began to trickle in during the coming hours as some of the bodies of our crew from Super 64 were eventually recovered from the savagery of the Somalis.

Later that day at the hospital in Landstuhl, I was taken down for more surgery prep and, beforehand, met with two doctors assigned to my case. My leg had been x-rayed and, as we looked at the image, I saw something more like pulverized rubble than a human bone. As they stared at the X-ray, the two doctors began to debate about various techniques they might employ, arguing between themselves. This did not give me great confidence, so I was finally relieved when they agreed to just do another debridement and pass me along, back through the system to specialists in the U.S.

One of the senior Army medics in the hospital talked to me for a while and gave me some of the best advice I have ever received. He explained that not all hospitals were the same, that there was a hierarchy, and that Walter Reed National Army Medical Center just outside Washington, D.C. was at the apex. He advised that, if given the choice, I should insist on being sent to Walter Reed.

After I came out of surgery and was back in my room, the doctors came in and informed me that flights to the U.S. were being scheduled. I was offered the choice of either going home to Georgia and being treated in the base hospital on Fort Benning or I could go to Walter Reed. I took the medic's advice and emphatically requested Walter Reed. It would mean remaining separated from Beth and my unit but, from what I had seen over the past week in the medical assessments of my leg, it would take every advantage and asset available to save it.

While still at Landstuhl Hospital waiting for medevac back to the States, all of the wounded Rangers were summoned to a meeting. Since arriving in Landstuhl, we had been kept in separate rooms and had not seen each other. I had been the only officer wounded in B Company and was the senior Ranger present at the meeting. It was a great relief to be back in the same room with other Rangers from my unit. Whether we fully realized it at the time or not, we had been welded together with bonds that went beyond just camaraderie and would last the rest of our lives. We continued to piece together information from the myriad parts of the battle until a lieutenant colonel came in and spoke up to start the meeting. He was accompanied by two young female captains. The lieutenant colonel said he was a Vietnam veteran and was now a psychologist. He told us that, as a group, we should continue to trade stories of the battle and describe what we had been through. Some of the Rangers were unable to hear, still deafened by the firefight. Most were in wheelchairs and all were heavily bandaged. As we talked, the stories of the intense fighting and details of our guys being hit, maimed, and killed began to spill out of the wounded Rangers. There was a lot of anger at the Somalis and lingering questions about why this had happened. Finally, as we began to wear out, the lieutenant colonel dismissed us. He later came by my room and I told him I hoped he hadn't gotten the wrong impression of us as soldiers based on some of the anger and brutal remarks. He waved me off, saying he completely understood. Then, with half a smile, he told me his two young assistants had already requested counselling for themselves, to help deal with the intensity of what they had heard as we talked about what we had experienced just days ago.

That week, we loaded another C-141 transport and departed Landstuhl for the United States. After a six-hour flight, we landed at Andrews Air Force Base in Maryland. When the tail ramp opened, Dave Grange, Jr. came on board to meet us. Newly promoted to brigadier general and stationed at the Pentagon, he had come over to welcome us home to the U.S. I was also surprised to see my cousin, Steve Lechner, a salty U.S. Navy command master chief, waiting to meet me as I was carried down the ramp of the aircraft. Steve was also stationed in Washington, D.C., and, like the rest of the nation, had seen the news of the battle. When he heard from my dad that I was in the fight and had been wounded, he immediately began to look for my name on the incoming flights before coming down to meet my plane. It was good to be back on U.S. soil and it meant a lot to see family. Soon, we were loaded into rickety military ambulances for the 45-minute trip to Walter Reed Army Medical Center. The bouncing vehicle jarred our wounds and made for an agonizing ride but we finally arrived at the large U.S. Army hospital inside the District of Columbia.

As the hospital began to sort out the relatively large influx of wounded, I was initially placed in a room with three other

Rangers. That was fine with me, and we drew strength from being together in a "fire team" as we continued to adjust from the shock in the aftermath of the battle.

Walter Reed Army Medical Center lived up to all I had heard and truly was the pinnacle of the military medical system. From the time we arrived, it was obvious we were in the best facility and being given the best care in the world for combat trauma. We had, not just one doctor or specialist per area, but teams of doctors and specialists. There was no indecision or argument but only resolution to use the most advanced techniques available to treat our wounds.

My team of orthopedic surgeons quickly resolved to use a relatively new technique that had been pioneered in Russia by a doctor named Ilizarov. Using this technique, a steel framework would be drilled into the remaining bone at the top and bottom portions of my lower right leg. The steel framework would be in the form of two rings encircling my leg, one above and one below the wound, and these would then be connected by vertical pieces. The framework would actually allow me to eventually bear weight on the leg, even with the 4-inch gap in the bone.

The first phase of my treatment would be to get the huge main wound and other holes in my leg closed and stabilized. Eventually, I underwent extensive surgery to have the Ilizarov device drilled in and placed on my leg. Then, the surgeons conducted major muscle and skin grafts to fill and close the holes. To fill the huge hole in my lower leg, the surgeons took half of my intact calf muscle from the back of the same leg and wrapped it around to the front. They then sealed it all up with skin grafts from my upper thigh. Stitches, pins, and more skin grafts closed the remainder of the wounds.

On my second day in the hospital, while preparations were underway to begin these surgeries, the nurse came into my room and said I had a visitor. Soon, my beautiful wife Beth was smiling at me and it was as if an angel had walked into the crowded, dark room. The Army had flown Beth up from Fort Benning to be with me just days after she had endured the tense drama of waiting through the mass casualty notifications in B Company. Throughout American history, after a battle, women have waited in dread for the delivery of a telegram or the uniformed officers knocking at the door. In the hours after the battle, Beth's vigil was broken by a phone call that I had been wounded. Things moved quickly from there and she was soon on a plane to join me in Washington, D.C. Not long after Beth came, my parents and sister arrived, having driven down from Rochester that same day. They were all there the next day when the Chief of Staff of the Army, General Gordon Sullivan, came over from the Pentagon to pin the Purple Heart medal on the hospital robe of each wounded Ranger.

I was soon moved to my own room and the hospital agreed to let Beth, now four months pregnant, stay in the room with me. We would spend the next six weeks together in Ward 57 of the orthopedic center. Having Beth with me, along with numerous visits and phone calls, especially from other wounded comrades, was a huge boost for my morale. I would need it as I now entered the next phase of my trials.

I had been repeatedly told along the way during my medical evacuation to keep my expectations low. If I kept my leg, I was told I would probably not be able to run or make full use of it again. I was determined that, if the surgeons could rebuild the basics of my leg, I would do the work to recover. While the medical staff were doing all they could for me, the treatment and recovery process was often agonizing and characterized by making gains, only to fall back and lose ground again. One of the worst parts of my treatment was the daily injection of powerful antibiotics administered to fight infection. Unfortunately, over time, these powerful chemicals destroyed the veins in both of my arms to the point there was nowhere left to put an IV needle. I then endured another surgery, which was performed to put a semi-permanent port in my chest for the injection of the chemical doses.

In those first days after our arrival at Walter Reed, the wounded Rangers were brought into a central room each morning to have our wounds unwrapped, cleaned, and inspected by our doctors. This was a necessary, but often torturous, process. After about a week of this our plastic surgeon, an excellent physician named Greg Antoine, came in one morning and jokingly said we probably wouldn't see him after today. It was a Thursday morning and he expected to get "orders overseas by Friday." Antoine had grown tired of watching our suffering with no acknowledgement from the Clinton Administration so, the previous day, he had called the White House to complain. The next day, Secretary of Defense Les Aspin arrived and came by each of our rooms. Two days later, on Sunday, Beth and I were awakened early by a hospital orderly and told that the President would be coming that morning. The reality of it did not really sink in for us until a Secret Service agent arrived to do a sweep of the room. About 30 minutes later, President Bill Clinton walked in without fanfare, quiet and somber. He thanked me for my service and sacrifice. Then, the White House photographer took pictures of us and President Clinton, which were later sent to us. This visit by our Commander in Chief, President Clinton, was among the greatest honors we received.

Along with the President, the wounded from Task Force Ranger had a number of other visitors at Walter Reed. On the Friday following the President's visit, Arnold Schwarzenegger took a break from filming a movie in Washington, D.C. and came to see each of the wounded Rangers. I had been a longtime fan of his movies and we talked about *Terminator* and *Conan* before he jumped into the bed with me for a picture.

My U.S. senator from the state of New York, Alfonse D'amato, visited and gave me a pair of congressional cufflinks. One of the most energetic and sincere visitors I had was Congressman Bob Dornan from California, who was also a former USAF fighter pilot. Dornan's visits began a few weeks after our arrival, when most of the attention was dying down. He came on many evenings after Congress was out of session and spent hours talking and encouraging us. On one visit, he presented each wounded Ranger with a U.S. flag he had personally flown in their honor over the U.S. Capitol. In the coming years, I would carry that same flag on every major deployment and operation I would take part in.

Congressman Dornan did more than just work behind the scenes. During those weeks, we watched him on CSPAN as he stood on the floor of Congress and railed against the bad decisions and poor leadership of the Clinton Administration. He spoke forcefully and in detail about how we had been sent to Mogadishu without the proper equipment and support. On one notable occasion, he talked about his visits to Walter Reed and mentioned each one of our names for entry into the Congressional Record.

As the weeks passed and many more visitors came through, my wounds slowly began to heal. In November, with my wounds now closed and leg stabilized in the Ilizarov device, I was allowed to temporarily return home to Fort Benning. After we had landed at the airport in Columbus outside of Fort Benning, my in-laws Jack and Caroline Jordan drove us to our house. Pulling into the driveway after months and a lifetime away, I saw the "Welcome Home" sign Beth's sister Martha had placed there, adorned with a yellow ribbon. She had also added the line "When Johnny Comes Marching Home," which reminded me I was joining the line of John Thomas Carson and the other Confederate heroes of their family. Not long after I had returned home,

I got a call from Bravo Company headquarters, which had also recently returned home from duty in Somalia. The message was an invitation to a memorial service for the fallen Rangers from Bravo Company.

As the rest of the company reestablished themselves back into the battalion, wounded Rangers were slowly returning to Fort Benning from various Army hospitals like Walter Reed. Bravo Company and the rest of the 3rd Ranger Battalion began to get back on track and continue the relentless training cycle. However, the effects of the deployment to Somalia with Task Force Ranger continued to weigh heavily, especially on the men of Bravo Company. As veterans have for millennia, formal actions were taken to incorporate and build upon the unit's legacy from Somalia. One of those formal actions was a memorial service for the six Rangers from Bravo Company who had been killed in Mogadishu. During the somber and tradition-filled ceremony, a momentous point came when Bravo Company First Sergeant Glenn Harris stepped forward and called the "roll" of the company. After the first sergeant called out the names of a number of Rangers present and they had answered with "here," the names of the fallen Rangers were called only to be met by deafening silence. The ceremony then continued with First Sergeant Harris leading all of the Rangers in reciting the Ranger Creed. As I stood leaning on my crutches in the assembled crowd with the rest of Bravo Company and many others, I was joined by Beth along with her uncle, William Storey, who had been an infantry officer in a Ranger company in Vietnam. As William and I, along with every Ranger present, echoed First Sergeant Harris and recited the Ranger Creed, I was again reminded that I was joining a long line of Rangers who had sacrificed in defense of this country since before its foundation.

After a few weeks back home in Columbus, as the healing progressed, I was soon able to get around fairly well on my crutches. I was also able to put weight on my leg with the help of the Ilizarov device holding things together. I continued to make good progress on my crutches, walking around my house and yard. However, there was much more treatment and reconstruction to do.

After spending the Thanksgiving and Christmas holidays with my family, I returned to Walter Reed for the next round of surgeries to continue rebuilding my leg. While the surgeons had been able to close the massive wounds, there still remained the problem of the 4-inch gap in my tibia or shin bone. My team of orthopedic surgeons decided to rebuild my leg using some extreme and near miraculous medical procedures. During hours of surgery, they started by opening my back near the waist. Then they hammered chunks out of my pelvis until they got enough bone material to pack in and fill the gap between the intact upper and lower parts of my tibia. Over time, the living bone would fuse with the material that had been packed into the gap, recalcifying and eventually completely absorbing it, creating new bone. While this miraculous process eventually succeeded, it was a tough surgery that not only included reopening my leg wound, but now my back and pelvis as well. It was successful, but left me unable to get out of bed again. With the new wounds in my back, I was restricted to lying on my side.

Throughout these weeks of progress and recovery, my wife Beth was at my side, helping me with the things I could not do. Against the backdrop of this burden, while we were at home at Fort Benning in March, she gave birth to our first daughter, Carolina. Just a few months later, I travelled back to Walter Reed one last time to have the Ilizarov device, with its steel spokes and framework, removed and my leg put in a cast. In another month, after returning to Fort Benning, the final and thirteenth surgery was performed to remove the port tube out of my chest. It had been eight long months since I had been wounded on the Mogadishu street and, though battered, my leg was healing well. The U.S. Army military medical teams had performed miracles. The muscle and skin grafts had closed the wounds and the bone was beginning to calcify, but there was still a long way to go.

I was buoyed by the progress being made but I still had other hurdles to clear. The muscles in my leg had severely atrophied, shriveling down to a fraction of their normal size and would take years to work back to anything approaching normal strength. A more subtle, and potentially more sinister, foe was that of the painkillers. After my first experience with morphine on the day I was wounded, I had been very careful to keep my use of the drug to a minimum.

Rather than use "hard drugs," I had relied on the allegedly more innocuous painkillers such as Percocet. After months on these painkillers, a friend half-jokingly asked if I was addicted. I considered that for a moment and realized I was taking up to at least two pills a day by that time. In reality, I was taking them more to "feel better" than to deal with pain. It had been a gradual, but slippery, slope to addiction. Taking immediate action to get off the Percocet, I spent a number of torturous nights trying to get my system and sleep patterns back under control. Fortunately, I was successful and it was not a more serious condition, but one that still affects me to this day in subtle ways, such as sleep loss.

With the removal of the Ilizarov device and the reconstruction of my leg taken as far as the masterfully skilled Army surgeons could take me, I was anxious to get into physical rehabilitation and get back on track as an infantry officer. It was now February of 1994, and while still recovering and making trips up to Walter Reed, I was notified by the 3rd Battalion headquarters that official orders had arrived for my promotion to captain. Hobbling on crutches to the front of a mass formation of both Alpha and Bravo companies in the battalion area, I had Beth and Lieutenant Colonel McKnight pin on my silver captain's bars. The promotion was mainly a matter of course, based upon having served my time as a lieutenant. However, the greatest honor for me was that my captain's bars were pinned on in front of two companies of my Ranger brothers. The promotion also served as a reminder that time was marching on and I would eventually have to get back onto my career path if I was to continue on in the Army.

During all of my medical treatments, I felt little to no bureaucratic pressure from the Army. The Army allowed my doctors and me as much time as necessary to ensure I healed. However, the clock was ticking on my career and I began to fall behind my peers. I needed to get into the Infantry Officers Advanced Course (IOAC) that I had originally been scheduled to attend the previous summer. With the help of my commanders at the 75th Ranger Regiment, I was able to get a slot to begin the course in June with a physical waiver due to still being on crutches. I would graduate from IOAC and go on to generally make a full recovery, continuing to serve in the infantry and airborne units for many more years and many other wars.

The year after I had been wounded was a long, arduous physical struggle to recover, exacerbated by numerous unforeseen difficulties and challenges. In spite of this, the skilled Army surgeons, my family, and especially my wife Beth had helped me push through and had literally gotten me back on my feet. Over many months, I worked hard to reach a point of near normalcy where I could walk, then slowly run, and at least start to rebuild myself as a soldier and infantry officer.

Most importantly, the Lord had answered my prayers. He had not only called me with near miraculous timing and circumstances to join B Company and Task Force Ranger, but had sustained me through the battle. He had brought me not only through the desperate fight, and home to see my family, but the struggle afterward to recover. I knew that there was a reason for not only my survival, but my perseverance, and the Lord had a continuing plan for me.

This belief was borne out through the 1990s as I deployed on a number of missions. The first was in command of an infantry rifle company during a six-month deployment and peacekeeping mission to the Sinai in Egypt. After company command, I returned to the 75th Ranger Regiment as a captain and from there was given a special mission. Still a member of the Ranger Regiment, I was detached for a year and deployed to Bosnia to serve as an operations officer in a special operations task force hunting war criminals.

But on September 11, 2001 my real destiny became apparent as the Global War on Terrorism began and I was called to deploy multiple times, taking up where we had left off, fighting and leading soldiers against Al Qaeda. Along with the military experience I would bring to these campaigns, one of the key lessons that I learned in the hospital at Walter Reed was that, although severely wounded, I was lucky as I would essentially recover with some scars. However, there are many other severely wounded soldiers who never fully recover. Amputees, quadriplegic and paraplegic paralyzed, and brain-injured soldiers may have their superficial wounds heal as I did, but they would never be able to fully recover as I had been fortunate and blessed to do. Soldiers with these injuries must endure the devastating physical results for the rest of their lives. Not only do the wounded soldiers suffer, but their families do as well. The families are the ones who acutely bear the burden of their sacrifice every day.

This experience and realization gave me a visceral appreciation and dedication to our catastrophically wounded veterans. My sister, Amy Tausch, who came with my parents to visit me in the first days after my arrival at Walter Reed, gained a similar perspective. She went on to form a nonprofit charity with her church called the New York Warrior Alliance, to support wounded veterans, the fallen, and their families. For almost two decades, they would travel to Walter Reed Army Medical Center and visit wounded soldiers in the hospital there from the current war. The New York Warrior Alliance continues to serve our wounded, their families, and Gold Star families to this day.

In the days following the battle in Mogadishu on October 3 and 4, reinforcements were called from the United States. These reinforcements included my old comrades from A Company, 3rd Ranger Battalion and another contingent of Delta operators. Additionally, more Regular U.S. Army units were sent, to include the armored vehicles that had originally been requested. Task Force Ranger focused its immediate efforts after the battle on recovering our lost comrades who had been taken from the crash site of Super 64. Eventually, bowing to intense diplomatic and military pressure and after suffering severely from the catastrophic losses inflicted during the early October battle, Aideed released Chief Warrant Officer Mike Durant and agreed to a ceasefire. However, in the meantime, the Clinton Administration decided the cost of "nation building" was too high. After Durant was returned and later the bodies of our lost comrades were recovered, the United States began to steadily scale down its efforts and withdraw from Somalia. But this was only temporary. After 9/11, the need to root out Al Qaeda's influence in Somalia was reidentified and the United States would return to continue its long war against radicals in the Horn of Africa. But long before the conflict with Al Qaeda was openly declared on 9/11, JSOC had begun to prepare.

Even before the operations of Task Force Ranger had ended in Mogadishu, JSOC had begun to carefully study the battle, distilling lessons learned, both good and bad, in its typically pragmatic fashion. JSOC would absorb these lessons, restructure its forces, and refine its methods. It would continue to build even better trained and coordinated teams out of the various special operations forces that must fight together. JSOC would also begin to comprehend the fact that effective special operations take more than just skilled warriors or "shooters." They also require intelligence systems, across multiple disciplines, capable of tracking any enemy, anywhere. This realization drove the development of a system of holistic planning and analysis, which is critical to guiding strike forces with precision. While limiting the impact of military operations on the civilian populace must be considered as part of the strategy, it was also determined that, once battle was joined, every conventional weapon available must be ruthlessly used to save the lives of American soldiers. The new systems and refocused units allowed JSOC to emerge eminently ready to begin devastating Al Qaeda immediately after the terrorist attacks on the United States in 2001.

Similarly, as a professional soldier and historian, I have long considered the lessons of Task Force Ranger in Mogadishu. At the time I deployed to Mogadishu, I had only been in the Army a few short years and lacked much of the perspective needed to grasp some of the difficulties that were involved in the formation of the task force and the conduct of its operations. Under a relatively new presidential administration, we were part of a military that was still coming to grips with the transition from the Cold War and massive conventional threat of the Soviet Union to the more asymmetric challenges of terrorism and insurgency that we were facing as the lone superpower.

There were many aspects of the employment of Task Force Ranger that were ill-conceived and ad hoc. We had a U.S. Navy anti-submarine plane as our primary airborne intelligence platform. While their crews were skilled professionals, they were unused to working for a ground combat force and there was little to no common understanding or unit cohesion between the two elements.

Similarly, cooperation with other assets in the overall U.S. intelligence network was not formalized and often inefficient. This was compounded by the fact we had been inserted into the relatively fragile structure of a United

Nations coalition that had not signed on, nor was it designed, for urban combat amidst a growing insurgency. Certainly, at the highest levels of command in the Pentagon and the presidential administration, there was a failure to grasp the complexities of tracking and pinpointing individual personalities like Aideed in a vast city, with a homogenous and hostile population. This was exacerbated by the administration's failure to realize that, while the confrontation between Aideed's Somali National Alliance and the UN may have begun as a personality-driven issue, it had quickly widened into a much larger conflict. By the summer of 1993, the large Habr Gidr clan and their allies, exhorted on by Aideed and enraged by UN attacks, were unified into all-out resistance. The Habr Gidr now perceived the conflict with the UN as a fight for the clan's survival amid the ghettos of their tribal areas. By the time Task Force Ranger arrived, the situation was past the point of possible success through a surgical removal of one or two leaders in the SNA. While what we would later call "high-value individual targeting" remains a valid approach, the situation in Mogadishu also called for more combat power. It was naïve of the senior leadership in Washington to think that the SNA did not have to be confronted on a larger scale and that the situation could be resolved by a clean and surgical raid on their higher leaders. Task Force Ranger had begun the inevitable process of taking down the network of the SNA leadership, but what was also required were regular combat units with armored vehicles and artillery to deal with the SNA throughout the city and allow better freedom of maneuver.

However, at the time, few of these issues resonated with us at the tactical level in the Ranger company, in the Delta assault teams or in the helicopter crews. We assumed that those above us, notably at the most senior levels, were taking a thorough and holistic look at the problem and doing their professional utmost to support our mission.

What absolutely did resonate with us all on the ground and in the air were the seeming half measures and the violations of time-honored mandates that all soldiers are taught. Among these are "Train as you fight," "Unity of effort," and having a clear and distinct chain of command. The ad hoc nature of the UN command, and even aspects of Task Force Ranger, were troubling even then and support seemed incomplete. By denying us the most lethal and capable aerial platforms, such as the AC-130, and substituting eager but unfamiliar assets, the senior leadership violated common sense on multiple levels.

Personal leadership and a clear chain of command are critical to the soldiers who are on the ground and in the fight. The old veterans of World War II, Korea, and modern battles like the Ia Drang in Vietnam had continued to pass these lessons on to us over the years and leading up to our deployment to Somalia. They were lessons written on the battlefield in the indelible ink of blood. Unlike most of our generation at that time, these older veterans had seen the maelstrom of battle and they knew that heavy combat and the ensuing chaos could cause events to sharply veer away from precisely planned operations and set timetables. While there were many shortfalls or things that were imperfect in the construct and conduct of operations during Operation *Gothic Serpent*, the training of the soldiers and tactical units who executed the missions was not among them.

Previously, I detailed aspects of training in the 75th Ranger Regiment and the utmost intent across U.S. special operations forces to achieve as much realism in training as possible. In this training approach, it is not acceptable to merely execute drills or redundant tasks by rote in a sterile environment. The standard of training is that, whenever the 75th Ranger Regiment is given a task or responsibility, the profile or steps for that mission and all of its inherent tasks must be run through completely in every aspect as closely as possible to reality. This includes the use of similar terrain, distances, and weather conditions. Live fire training with Rangers using all of their weapons and firing real ammunition is the central pillar of this approach.

This type of training and the intensity of the cultural environment in the 75th Ranger Regiment is not for everyone. It takes not only a tough soldier, but a smart and disciplined one as well. To ensure the right soldiers are in the line units of the 75th Ranger Regiment, a long and methodical process of weeding out the chaff occurs from the first day a future Ranger enters the Army. It continues on, growing more intense as he passes through the various stages of training, to include Airborne School and 75th

Ranger Regiment's Assessment Program until finally arriving at his unit, ready to join the team. This is where his real training begins, and no effort is spared to ensure that everyone on the team can perform exactly as he needs to in combat.

Along the same lines, but at the highest level of military skill, I have made brief mention of the methodical, extensive, and intensive training that goes into selecting and training an individual Delta operator. Similarly, the assault teams and various echelons of a Delta squadron receive extensive training as well. In Mogadishu, the performance of the individual Delta operators once again completely validated the system, selectivity, and vast amounts of training and resources they received. But their employment and some of the approaches of the task force in Mogadishu bore scrutiny.

No amount of planning or support can guarantee that a raid will go smoothly. It may not be possible on every mission to achieve complete surprise or bring overwhelming force to a target. The enemy becomes a critical factor in any mission planning. When a resolute enemy fights, they "get a vote" on the plan and stand up combat is often unavoidable. Given those realities, teamwork and unit cohesion are critical and the ad hoc nature of a task force must be absolutely minimized. The "pick up team" approach should not be permitted in mission critical areas. This means that Delta or the special operations task force must possess some degree of its own capability, as well as its own people and resources, to perform the tasks required to get the mission done. The 160th were more than adequate for air movement and fire support. However, the airborne intelligence and surveillance assets must reside permanently on the team as well. Mobility is another key, and Delta and the Rangers of a task force must be able to get in and out, in armored vehicles if necessary, without relying on any outside unit. Along the same lines, the aperture of Delta's focus must widen to a degree beyond surgical hostage rescue or prisoner snatch, incorporating the ability to fight their way in and out as well.

I have previously described how magnificent the pilots of the 160th were who flew in our task force. This performance once again was the byproduct of selecting the right people and pushing them to their utmost capability with intense, realistic training. Secondarily, it was the result of having some of the greatest helicopters and equipment in the world.

Just as training is important, leadership is possibly the single most significant factor in an effective combat unit. There was no lack of leadership in Task Force Ranger at any level. Inherent to the training of every unit involved in Task Force Ranger was the constant admonition to take charge of the situation around you and push on toward the goal of mission success, no matter what that may be or what challenges confront you. While the chain of command tried to sort through the chaos and complexities of the battle, the individual Ranger, Delta operator, and 160th pilot made sure the piece of ground they held or airspace they were in was secured properly and, if necessary, gave orders to those around them.

All of these factors played into the other key aspect of our mission success, which was morale. I have spoken of the confidence each of us had in each other and the other parts of the team. We knew that we were going to hold our corner or piece of ground at all costs and that those to the left, right, and above us were doing the same. As a soldier and combat veteran, I have personally experienced, to varying degrees, many of the aspects of the different types of campaigns, battles, and military operations that I have read about in history, with one notable exception. I have never experienced being in a unit that has broken under the pressure of the enemy.

The assault force fighting around the crash site of Super 61 certainly felt immense pressure from the enemy as waves of Somali gunmen relentlessly closed in on us and thousands more pressed in from the nearby crowds and surrounding city. But never for a moment did the men of Task Force Ranger waver, take a step back or begin to show signs of breaking. Part of the reason for this was our training. But the overriding factor was the immense confidence we had in each other, underlining a determination that, no matter what came, we would never quit, give up or run. That level of cohesion and high morale is a rare thing on the battlefield and an amazing honor to be a part of.

274

EPILOGUE

Today, as I write this 30 years after the battle in Mogadishu, it almost seems like a dream. But it is a dream that often reaches into my daily consciousness. After numerous other battles and countless missions over the past decades, especially during the wars in Iraq and Afghanistan, my experiences in Mogadishu sometimes start to fade and recede into the background. But then I will look down at my heavily scarred leg or, in a quiet moment, watch the blades on a ceiling fan for too long, and the dust and blood in the streets and orbiting helicopters come back to me in a rush.

For the rest of my days in the United States Army, I wore the scroll of 3rd Ranger Battalion on the right shoulder of my uniform in accordance with the prescribed standard custom and regulation for combat veterans. Of all the badges, patches, and awards I received in the Army, there was none I wore more proudly. Many years after Somalia, in 2006 and 2007, I served a 15-month tour in Iraq with a brigade of the 1st Armored Division as its deputy commander. In the spring of 2006, as part of the military "surge" of additional forces, our brigade was ordered to the city of Ramadi, amid some of the hardest fighting of the long Iraq war. During those battles, the young officers and sergeants would occasionally ask me about Mogadishu and I would respond that it was like our year-long tour in Ramadi, only compressed into 18 hours.

Task Force Ranger was not perfect. We made mistakes and had internal frictions that, in retrospect, were petty and often contrary to everything we had been trained on as professional soldiers. The crucible of battle will always reveal the weak links and a few were identified that day. As on every battlefield, there were soldiers who failed in combat or shirked their duty. There were others who made bad decisions that endangered their comrades. However, these were incredibly few and, nearly to a man, the soldiers on the ground and in the air with Task Force Ranger were utterly dedicated, eager for the mission, and absolutely ready for any fight that may have come. When, against all expectations, that fight was thrust upon us and became a desperate struggle, the intensity of devotion, heroism, and displays of valor stand out in the history of the U.S. military and have become an inspiration and enduring legend. Among the many battles in American history in which our soldiers have fought with astonishing skill and valor, Mogadishu has taken its place in a pantheon of honor.

The battle in Mogadishu in 1993 was America's first direct confrontation with Al Qaeda. Led by Osama bin Laden, this same enemy would later slither back into the nation's consciousness, renewing the blood feud on September 11, 2001. While the battle in Mogadishu had been a tactical success, it had not been without losses and mistakes. These experiences and lessons, however, undoubtedly helped prepare Joint Special Operations Command and its forces for the coming battles in the next rounds of the fight and for the coming crusade against Islamic extremists known as the Global War on Terrorism.

I was honored to serve in many more special operations task forces after Mogadishu, as well as with many conventional units during the Global War on Terrorism. I would experience more long days and nights of battle and I would lose many more friends, but I would also experience great victories during this later war. After being wounded in Mogadishu and nearly losing my leg, I would return to the infantry, thanks to the incredible doctors at Walter Reed Army Medical Center. After my recovery, I would go on to command an infantry rifle company and lead it on a six-month deployment during peacekeeping operations in Sinai, Egypt. Following that, I would also return to the 75th Ranger Regiment. Incredibly, after being wounded, I was eventually able to not only run and road march, but also parachute on my reconstructed right leg. It was during this second tour assigned to the 75th Ranger Regiment in 1999 that I deployed to Bosnia. There, in the former Yugoslavia with another special operations task force, I was able to put to use many of the more subtle lessons learned during our operations in Somalia and the search for Aideed. For the Bosnia mission, our task force was under the command of NATO and made up of allies and special operators from Germany, France, the UK, and the Netherlands. These nations were all working together in the task force to hunt war criminals in the former Yugoslavia from its civil war in the 1990s. In 1999, I served as the J3 operations officer for the task force. It was a job that would cause me to relive, on numerous occasions, many of the complex problems of trying to locate individual targets on their home ground. But during this deployment in Bosnia, U.S. special operations forces were also able to refine our skills, aided by intelligence and law enforcement professionals, using sophisticated and subtle approaches in addition to direct military action. With great satisfaction, our special operations task force in Bosnia captured numerous brutal criminals and their senior leaders. These missions in Bosnia in the late 1990s, along with our experiences during the Somalia operations, began to set the stage and develop the immense capability that would soon be called on in defense of the nation following the terrorist attacks of September 11, 2001.

The challenge that the Global War on Terrorism brought to every professional soldier was of a scope and duration that we could not then imagine on 9/11 as the drums of war sounded in the wake of the attacks on New York City and Washington, D.C. Years of deployments to the wars in Iraq and Afghanistan, with scores of combat operations in those countries and many others, brought not only successful missions and great victories but challenging days and heartbreaking losses. In Iraq, we would fight Al Qaeda in the rubble of cities while simultaneously breaking the code of counter-insurgency with the tribes. We tried to repeat those successes in Afghanistan and experienced many more battles on lonely mountainsides. The memories of these campaigns and the many comrades I had there live in me still. They are all threads in the story and the tapestry that began to be woven and spun even before my first arrival at Fort Benning. But for me, running prominently among these threads of memory is Somalia.

October 3 and the battle in Mogadishu remains one of the greatest days of my life. I do not use those terms loosely or to imply that it was all positive, but to illustrate the monumental nature and impact the battle had on my life. Of the numerous battles I have been in since that time, none has matched Mogadishu for sheer intensity. That intensity resulted in not only horrible and crushing losses but also incredible acts of valor and devotion. I am personally indebted to many members of Task Force Ranger, foremost among them Delta operators Bart Bullock, who risked his life to pull me in from the fire-swept street, and Norm Hooten, who took vengeance on the Somali gunman who shot me. The entire force on the ground owes a debt to our pilots who, in spite of the odds and having that day witnessed five of their own aircraft shot down, never left us during the fight. Especially of note: Hal Wade, Randy Jones, Chuck Harrison, and the rest of the gunship pilots who showed both stunning bravery and self-restraint as they held their fire, at incredible risk to themselves, to ensure our safety before devastating the enemy and giving us room to breathe and, ultimately, survive.

The former commander of U.S. Special Operations Command and a fellow Ranger, General Wayne Downing, borrowed from accounts of the World War II battle of Iwo Jima to aptly describe Task Force Ranger, quoting, "Uncommon valor was a common virtue." There is no more accurate description of Task Force Ranger during the battle in Mogadishu. While I remain in awe of the valor and determination of the warriors around and above me that day, what continues to impress me most is the enduring bond that is unique to a small group who, when faced with adversity and overwhelming odds, stands together and takes on all that comes. My personal experience in life has been that people and human institutions will eventually fail you. The only thing I can place my absolute faith in is the Lord, Jesus Christ. But along with Him, my spirit will always hold fast to the brotherhood of the men of Task Force Ranger.

> We few, we happy few, we band of brothers;
> For he to-day that sheds his blood with me
> Shall be my brother; be he ne'er so vile,
> This day shall gentle his condition;
> And gentlemen in England now a-bed
> Shall think themselves accurs'd they were not here,
> And hold their manhoods cheap whiles any speaks
> That fought with us upon Saint Crispin's day.[*]

[*] William Shakespeare, *Henry V* (New York: Simon and Schuster, 2020).

INDEX

9/11 attacks 267, 268, 276–77, 278

75th Ranger Rgt 44–45, 50, 54–55, 56, 98–99
  1st Btn 72, 73
  3rd Btn 62–63, 69–75
  and Aideed 146–47
  and black missions 94–95
  and Bosnia 277–78
  and casualties 243–55
  and Creed 68–69
  and deployment 82–83
  and *Gothic Serpent* training 128–30, 131–35
  and Grange 81–82
  and Grenada 69–70
  and helicopter assaults 87–90
  and operations orders 111–12
  and Orientation Program 65–67
  and parachute assaults 83–86
  and promotion 263–64
  and Ranger Ready Force (RRF) 101–3
  and target 152–57
  and training 86–87, 271–72
  see also Alpha Company; Bravo Company

Adeere, Sheik Aden 197
Advanced Infantry Training 40–41, 46

Afghanistan 176, 278–79
Aideed, Mohamed Farah 19, 115, 116, 117–18, 180–81
  and ceasefire 266–67
  and hunt 144–48, 158, 160–61, 163, 165–66
  and Italy 167, 168
  and Al Qaeda 175–76
aircraft, U.S. 128–29
  AC-130 gunship 75, 77, 86, 93, 123–24, 135, 136
  C-5; 139–40
Alpha Company 71, 72, 73, 74, 75, 76–81
  and deployment 105–6, 107, 108–11, 112–13
  and RRF 103
  and training 92–94
American Civil War (1861–65) 31–32, 92, 95–96
Antoine, Greg 257–58
armored vehicles 40, 60, 136, 230
Army National Guard 20, 25, 45–46, 75
Aspin, Les 135, 258
Atto, Osman 157, 168–74, 176

Baidao 99
Bakara Market 180–81
Barre, Mohamed Siad 116
Beckwith, Col Charlie 144

Bin Laden, Osama   175–76, 181,
  196–97, 276
black missions   82, 94–95
Blackburn, Pvt 1C Todd   191–92,
  237
Blackhawks *see* helicopter assaults
Boorn, S/Sgt Kenny   189, 190
Bosnia   265, 277–78
Boy Scouts   27–28
Boykin, Col Jerry   127, 136, 143,
  158, 182, 250
Bravo Company   76–77, 104,
  118–27, 260–61
  and deployment   107, 108–9,
  137–40
  and training   159–60
Bray, T/Sgt Jeff   121
Breen, Lt John   149, 173
Briley, Donovan   172, 194, 241
British Parachute Rgt   86
Bullock, Sgt/1C Bart   192, 214–15,
  279
Busch, Dan   177, 194–96
Bush, George H.W.   61, 99

Camp Darby   52–53, 54
Carlson, Pvt 1C Chris   225
Carson, Maj John Thomas   92, 259
Cash, Sgt Raleigh   234, 244
Cashen, Steve   139
Cavaco, Corp James   224–25
Charleston (SC)   29, 30–31, 32, 42
Charlie Company   76–77
Churchill, Winston   106
Citadel, The (SC)   29–34, 36–39
  and chapel   43–44
  and graduation   46–48
  and professors   42–43
  and training   44–46
  and upperclassmen   41–42

Cleveland, Sgt Bill   129, 184, 217
Clinton, Bill   18, 99, 115, 117, 258
cohesion   35–36
Columbus (GA)   76
Combat Search and Rescue
  (CSAR)   121, 124–25
Combat Support Hospitals
  (CSHs)   245–50
Commandos   86
communism   59–60, 70, 82
convoys *see* vehicle convoys
Custer, Gen George   95–96

D'amato, Alfonse   258
Darby, Brig Gen William O.   52, 69
defensive fighting   40–41
Delta   94–95, 109, 110–11, 112,
  113–15
  and Garrison   144
  and Mogadishu   118, 119–20,
  121–27
  and target   155
  and training   272–73
Dervishes   100
desert conditions   57, 88
Dick, Lt Col Harvey   43
discipline   35–36, 43
DiTomasso, Lt Tom   194, 195, 207
Donovan, "Doc"   89
Dornan, Bob   258–59
Downing, Gen Wayne   280
Dugway (UT)   57, 88–90
Durant, Mike   94, 129, 153, 177
  and capture   251
  and crash   217, 218, 219, 220,
  221–22
  and release   266, 267

Eglin Air Force Base (FL)   54–56
Egyptian forces   149–50, 233

equipment 131
Eversmann, Sgt Matt 191–92

famine 18, 116
Fields, Sgt Tom 129, 217
Fillmore, Earl 206
fire supporters 50, 75, 78, 80–81,
    120–21
FM radios 122–23
food 54, 56, 99, 164
Fort Benning (GA) 20, 21–24,
    25–26, 39–41, 46
  and 75th Ranger Rgt 71–75
  and casualties 259–60
  and Orientation Program 65–67
  and Ranger School 52–54,
    56–57
Fort Bliss (TX) 20, 102–3, 137
Fort Bragg (NC) 20, 46, 108–13
Fort Campbell (KY) 92–93
Fort Sill (OK) 49–50, 51–52
forward observers (FOs) 50
Fourth Class system 34, 35–36,
    37–39, 47
Frank, Ray 129, 153, 217, 218

Gallagher, Sgt 1C Bob 228–29,
    232, 233
Galliete, Sgt Butch 103, 106, 107,
    121, 137
  and CSAR 125
  and raids 196, 198
Galloway, Joe 95
Garrison, Maj Gen Bill 143–44,
    151, 158, 162
  and raids 182, 183–84
Germany 58, 250–54
Global War on Terrorism 265,
    277, 278–79
Goffena, Mike 218, 220

Goodale, Sgt Mike 187–88, 190,
    202
Gordon, M/Sgt Gary 218–19,
    220–21, 229
GPS navigation 76
Grange, Brig Gen Dave, Jr. 81–83,
    86, 90, 98–99, 254
Grenada 25, 45, 73
  and Urgent Fury 69–70, 78, 127
Grimsley, Maj Gen James A. 46–47
Gundel, Herr 43
"Gunsmoke" exercise 93–94

Habr Gidr clan 17–18, 19–20, 117,
    151, 269
  and Aideed 147
  and dissenters 144–45
  and Italy 167
Hall, Mike 45
Halling, Brad 218, 219–20
Harosky, Joe 162
Harp, Jerry 212
Harrell, Lt Col Gary 114, 115,
    118, 119, 120, 126
  and crash 237
  and Mogadishu 143
  and raids 192
Harris, 1/Sgt Glenn 107, 108, 152,
    177–78
  and memorial 260, 261
Harrison, Chuck 212, 217, 279
Hartley, Sgt Mark 79
heat conditions 143
helicopter assaults 67, 78, 87–90
  and Atto 172–73
  and Bakara Market 184–87
  and call signs 126
  and crash sites 194–96, 197–98,
    199–201, 218–23, 236–37, 241,
    251–52

and Lig Ligato House 152–58
and Mogadishu 118–22
and Russian Compound 160–63
and street fighting 207–18
and training 129–30, 131–35
Henderson, David 29–30
Hitler Youth 27
HMMV trucks 17–18, 162–63, 193
Hooten, Sgt Norm "Hoot" 210,
215, 250, 279
humanitarian aid 99, 116
hypothermia 55

Indian Army 166–67
Infantry Officers Advance Course
(IOAC) 101, 264
intelligence 144–47, 151, 267,
268–69
and Aideed 160
and Atto 168–69, 170
and Italian Army 167
see also spies
Iran 73, 81, 127
Iraq 60–61, 65, 72, 73, 88
and War on Terror 275–76,
278–79
Islam 100
Italian Army 150, 167–68

Japan 59
Jenkins, Micah 48
Jennings, Mike 28–29, 76
Joint Special Operations Command
(JSOC) 77, 109, 144, 267–68
Jollota, Dan 196
Jones, Randy 209, 212, 216–17,
279
Joyce, Sgt Casey 178, 224
Jumpmaster School 80
jungle conditions 78

Kenneally, Lt Col John 88–89,
98
Kinderer, Tony 209–10
Kismayo 99
Klingaman, Capt Jim 91, 97–98,
112–13, 151, 173
and surveillance 180, 181, 183
Knight, Rick 45
Korea see North Korea; South Korea
Kowalewski, Pvt 1C Richard
227–28
Kuhlsrude, Larry 209–10
Kurth, Mike 188
Kuwait 60–61, 62, 72, 73

Lamb, Sgt/1C Al 125, 197
Lamb, Sgt/1C Rick 231, 236,
243–44
Lance missile units 58
laser designators 76
leadership 273–74
leave 91
Lechner, Beth 89–90, 91–92, 97,
101, 102, 256–57, 262
and phone calls 178
Lechner, Carolina 262
Lechner, Steve 254
Lee, Robert E. 32, 92
Leon-Guerrero, Sgt Maj Mariano
("LG") 74–75, 86
Lessner, Sgt Wayne 103, 106, 107,
137
Lig Ligato House 151–58
Lincoln, Abraham 31

McKnight, Lt Col Danny 97–98,
104, 105, 108–9
and media 146
and Mogadishu 143
and raids 192

and Russian Compound 162
and street fighting 223–24,
  228–29, 232
McLaughlin, Sgt Jeff 189
Maddox, John 225–26
Maier, Karl 195, 220
Malaysian forces 235, 241, 242
Marsh, Maj John "Doc" 134, 137
Martin, M/Sgt Tim "Griz" 225,
  226, 227
Matthews, Lt Col Tom 119–20,
  126, 192
media 146, 158
Middle East see Iran; Iraq
military academies 30–34, 36
militias 99–100, 147–48, 150; see
  also Somali National Alliance
Mogadishu 17–18, 99, 100,
  275–76, 279–80
  and Aideed 117–18
  and airfield 141–43, 149–51,
    176–77
  and helicopter assaults 118–27
  and lessons 276–77
  and Lig Ligato House 151–58
  and raids 180–97
  and Russian Compound 160–63
  and SNA 165–66
  and street fighting 200–17
  and vehicle convoys 222–29,
    230–36, 238–42
Moore, Lt Gen Hal 95–97, 120
morale 274
mountain conditions 51, 53, 67,
  78
movements to contact 78

NATO 277–78
Neathery, Pete 204
New York Warrior Alliance 266

Nigerian forces 19
night missions 133, 238–39
Nixon, Maj Craig 71–72, 148–49
  and convoys 229, 230, 231–32,
    234
Noriega, Manuel 54
North Korea 59–60, 82
North Vietnamese Army
  (NVA) 96

operations:
  Desert Shield (1990–91) 61–62,
    82
  Desert Storm (1991) 94
  Eagle Claw (1980) 73, 81, 127
  Gothic Serpent (1993) 128
  Just Cause (1989) 70, 74
  Urgent Fury (1983) 69–70
Othic, Clay 227

Pakistani forces 17, 19, 167, 235,
  243
Palmer, Sgt Jeffrey 87
Palmer, Milton 55–56
Panama 54, 56–57, 70, 210
  and veterans 73, 78–79, 94, 127
parachute assaults 59, 73, 78, 80,
  83–86
peacekeeping missions 99, 265
Pellerin, Sgt Mark 79
Perino, Lt Larry 153, 161, 182–83
phalanx formation 34–35
Pilla, Spc Dominic 193
planning 111–12
Plumley, Sgt Maj Basil 95, 96–97
Pringle, Sgt Mike 162–63

Al Qaeda 175–76, 181, 196–97,
  217, 265, 267, 268
  and Iraq 276–77, 278–79

radio   76, 122–23, 126, 144, 147
raids   78, 90–91, 117–21, 169–74
Ramaglia, Sgt Randy   237
Ranger Creed   68–69
Ranger School   50–51, 52–57,
    67–68
Reagan, Ronald   39
reconnaissance helicopters   145,
    149, 180
refugees   99, 116
religion   43–44, 106–7, 264–65
Rentz, USS   163–65
Reserve Officers Training Corps
    (ROTC)   44–45, 46
Rochester (NY)   26–30
Rodriguez, Spc Adalberto
    "Rod"   225, 226
Rodriguez, Spc Carlos   189
Ruiz, Sgt Lorenzo   226–27
Russell, Maj Ron   127–28
Russian Compound   160–63
Ryswyk, Lt Lee   177, 182

Saddam Hussein   60–61, 73, 82
Saudi Arabia   61
Schwarzenegger, Arnold   258
Sherman, Gen William T.   32
shields   34–35
Shughart, Sgt 1C Randy   219,
    220–21, 229
Siegfried, Col Steve   24
signals intelligence (SIGINT)   144,
    147
signature flights   159
Sinai (Egypt)   265, 277
Sizemore, Spc Dale   231
Smith, Sgt Brian   79
Smith, Chris   212
Smith, Corp Jamie   189, 238–39
Smith, Jim   195, 198

SNA see Somali National Alliance
snipers   121–22, 177
Somali National Alliance
    (SNA)   18–19, 146, 269–70
  and Bakara Market   181
  and Durant   221–22
  and hunt   165–66
  and Italy   167–68
  and target   151, 157
  see also Atto, Osman
Somalia   99–100, 103–4, 116–18,
    267–71
  and ceasefire   266–67
  and Delta   114–16
  and mission restraint   135–36
  and training   159–60
  see also Mogadishu
South America   82
South Carolina   10, 29, 30, 31–32
South Korea   58–60, 61–62, 75,
    90–91
Soviet Union   58, 82, 146, 148, 167,
    176
Sparta   34–35
Spaulding, Sgt   226
Spellmeyer, Lt Scott   231
spies   144, 160, 180–81, 183
Stauss, Lt Col Ken   88
Steele, Capt Mike   107–8, 110–11,
    112, 113, 127
  and Atto   169
  and beach   179, 180
  and raids   182–83, 187, 191, 194
  and Russian Compound   161
  and street fighting   202, 206, 207,
    209, 213–14, 237
  and target   151, 152, 153, 154,
    156
Storey, William   260–61
Straight, Sgt Jerry   79

Strous, "Doc" 204

Strueker, S/Sgt Jeff 192–93, 222–23, 237

Sudan 196–97

Sullivan, Gen Gordon 256

Suranski, Pvt Eric 205

surveillance 151, 165, 169, 173, 180–81

swamp conditions 51–53, 54–55, 57, 78

target building *see* Lig Ligato House

Tausch, Amy 266

terrorism 82, 176, 196; *see also* 9/11 attacks

Thomas, Spc Joe 189, 190–91, 207–8, 212, 244

Thomas, Sgt Keni 204–5, 213

training 23–24, 25–26, 39–41, 271–73

and 75th Ranger Rgt 82–83, 86–87

and Alpha Company 92–94

and artillery 49–50, 51–52

and Bravo Company 159–60

and fire supporters 80–81

and *Gothic Serpent* 128–30, 131–35

and helicopter assaults 88–90

and parachute assaults 80

and Ranger companies 76–78

and Ranger School 52–57, 67–68

and ROTC 44–45, 46

and RRF 102–3

trench lines 40–41

Tyler, Lyon G. 43

UHF radios 122–23

uniforms 130–31, 143

United Nations (UN) 99

United Nations (UN) forces 17, 18–20, 116–17

and airfield 149–50

and coalition 166–68

and convoys 235–36

and intelligence 145, 146

and QRF 174–75

and urban combat 269

United States of America (USA) 18, 26–30, 91–92

and black missions 94–95

and Iraq 61

and mission restraint 135–36

and Panama 56

and Somalia 99–100, 116–17, 267

unmanned aerial vehicles (UAVs) 76

urban combat 200–17, 269–70

U.S. Air Force 56, 75

and C-141 transports 83–86

and Combat Control Teams (CCTs) 121, 122

and helicopter assaults 88–89

and Pararescuemen (PJs) 125, 197

U.S. Army 17–18, 19–20, 39–40

and casualties 265–66

and lessons 267–71

and medics 245–46, 249–50, 252

and Rangers 24–25, 76–79

and Somalia 99, 103–4, 116

see also Citadel, The; Delta; Fort Benning (GA); Ranger School

U.S. Army (units):

1st Armored Dvn 275–76

2nd Infantry Dvn 57–58, 59–60

10th Mountain Dvn 148, 149, 151, 174–75

82nd Airborne Dvn 61–63, 79

160th SOAR Rgt   93–94, 102,
  103, 115, 273
503rd Infantry Rgt   58–59
1st Btn/7th Cavalry Rgt   95–97
see also 75th Ranger Rgt
U.S. Army Field Artillery School
  (OK)   48, 49–50, 51–52
U.S. Marine Corps   26, 49, 75, 86,
  116
U.S. Navy   75, 163–65
  P-3 Orion   144, 145, 268

vehicle convoys   124, 133, 192–93,
  200
  and street fighting   222–29,
  230–36, 240–42
Vietnam War (1955–75)   24, 25, 75,
  95–97, 120

Wade, Hal   208, 209, 212, 216–17,
  279
Walter Reed National Army Medical
  Center (D.C.)   252–53, 254–59,
  261–62, 266

Washington, George   26, 92
Watson, Sgt/1C Sean   189, 190, 191
  and street fighting   202, 203–4,
  205, 209
We Were Soldiers Once and Young
  (Galloway/Moore)   95
weaponry, Somali   162, 175, 176
weaponry, U.S.   50, 76–77
  and grenades   197–98
  and helicopters   87–88
  M16A2 rifle   24, 40
  and vehicle convoys   124
weather conditions   55–56, 60
White, Paul   212
Williams, Arland D.   29
Wolcott, Cliff   154, 156, 157–58,
  177, 241
  and Atto   172
  and raids   191, 193–94
World War II (1939–45)   43,
  46–47, 52, 59, 69, 240

Yacone, Jim   218
Young, Pvt 1C Jeff   189